NO LC
SEA

D0501886

Thank YOU

This book
purchased
with donations
made to the
GiveBIG
for Books
Campaign.

The
Seattle
Public
Library
Foundation

www.foundation.spl.org

Received on:

FEB 2 6 2014

Green Lake Library

Praise for Lu Ann Cahn's

I DARE ME

"I love the bold and brave spirit of this book—along with its wit, warmth, honesty, and endearing sense of fearless self-deprecation. In these pages, the author has packed not only a year of courage, but more than enough for a lifetime. I think (and hope) that her journey will inspire many others like it!"

—Elizabeth Gilbert, author of *Eat, Pray, Love* and
The Signature of All Things

"I loved Lu Ann Cahn's *I Dare Me*! This is a book that can change your life—if you let it. Her Year of Firsts inspired me, as does the story of her life! A must-read for every woman I know."

—Lisa Scottoline, *New York Times* bestselling author

"Lu Ann Cahn has written a delightful and helpful guide to all the ways large and small to unstick your life. Even if you don't want to eat a grasshopper."

—Delia Ephron, author of *Sister Mother Husband Dog*

"*I Dare Me* is hilariously inspiring. This book will motivate you to step out of your comfort zone and take more life-changing chances to increase your life fulfillment and happiness quotient! You will fall in love with Lu Ann's charm and story-telling style, which is not just entertaining but empowering to say the least!"

—Jen Groover, author of *What If? & Why Not?*

"First First? Buy this book. Then take in Cahn's spirit and try out her plan. It can only do you good."

—Judith Sills, PhD, author of
The Comfort Trap, or What If You're Riding a Dead Horse

continued . . .

"Everyone needs a best friend like Lu Ann Cahn—the bold, spontaneous, zany-in-a-good-way friend—who dares you to do what you would never otherwise consider but makes it look so fun you just have to give it a go. You might curse her name while up on that mechanical bull, but you'll end up thanking her for shaking up your life. Packed with laughter, shrieking, and the thrill of the new, *I Dare Me* is an irresistible guide to making every day an adventure."

—Patty Chang Anker, author of
Some Nerve: Lessons Learned While Becoming Brave

"Lu Ann Cahn has taken the concept of 'falling into a rut' and conquered it in the most humorous and accessible way. From plunging into the ocean on New Year's Day to eating desserts all day long, she made her year of 'Firsts' into a guide for anyone who needs to recharge, reboot, and find the joy in the quotidian."

—Ellen Lubin-Sherman, author of *The Essentials of Fabulous*

I DARE ME

How I Rebooted and Recharged My Life
by Doing Something New Every Day

LU ANN CAHN

A PERIGEE BOOK

A PERIGEE BOOK
Published by the Penguin Group
Penguin Group (USA) LLC
375 Hudson Street, New York, New York 10014

USA • Canada • UK • Ireland • Australia • New Zealand • India • South Africa • China

penguin.com

A Penguin Random House Company

Copyright © 2013 by Lu Ann Cahn
Penguin supports copyright. Copyright fuels creativity, encourages diverse voices,
promotes free speech, and creates a vibrant culture. Thank you for buying an authorized
edition of this book and for complying with copyright laws by not reproducing, scanning,
or distributing any part of it in any form without permission. You are supporting writers
and allowing Penguin to continue to publish books for every reader.

PERIGEE is a registered trademark of Penguin Group (USA) LLC.
The "P" design is a trademark belonging to Penguin Group (USA) LLC.

Library of Congress Cataloging-in-Publication Data

Cahn, Lu Ann.
I dare me : how I rebooted and recharged my life by doing something new every day / Lu Ann Cahn.
pages cm
Includes bibliographical references.
ISBN 978-0-399-16167-4 (hardback)
1. Self-actualization (Psychology)   2. Self-esteem.   3. Happiness.   I. Title.
BF637.S4C314   2013
646.7—dc23   2013020113

First edition: November 2013

PRINTED IN THE UNITED STATES OF AMERICA

10 9 8 7 6 5 4 3 2 1

Text design by Laura K. Corless

This book describes the real experiences of real people. The author has disguised the
identities of some, and in some instances created composite characters, but none of these
changes has affected the truthfulness and accuracy of her story. Penguin is committed to
publishing works of quality and integrity. In that spirit, we are proud to offer this book to our
readers; however, the story, the experiences, and the words are the author's alone.

While the author has made every effort to provide accurate telephone numbers, Internet
addresses, and other contact information at the time of publication, neither the publisher
nor the author assumes any responsibility for errors, or for changes that occur after publication.
Further, the publisher does not have any control over and does not assume any
responsibility for author or third-party websites or their content.

Most Perigee books are available at special quantity discounts for bulk purchases for sales promotions,
premiums, fund-raising, or educational use. Special books, or book excerpts, can also be created to fit
specific needs. For details, write: Special.Markets@us.penguingroup.com.

Dedicated to
my daughter, Alexa, who inspires me
my husband, Phil, who believes in me
my mother, Carol Berman, who taught me
to live life as an adventure

CONTENTS

INTRODUCTION

In August 2012, at a Philadelphia restaurant, ten-year-old Cleo, my friend's niece, sat across from me and asked, "What are you writing about?"

Her uncle Andrew had told her I was "an author."

"I'm writing about a Year of Firsts. Every day for a year I did something new."

Cleo's eyes got big.

"Every single day?"

"Uh-huh."

"Like what? What did you do?"

"Oh, let's see . . . I ate a scorpion."

"Ewwwwwwww." Cleo wrinkled her freckled nose.

"I zip-lined across a lake filled with alligators!"

"WHAT?? Really?"

"Yep. I learned to Hula-Hoop."

"I can do that." Cleo wasn't impressed with that one.

"What do you want to do for the first time?" I asked her.

"Eat escargot!" she said precociously. Everyone at the table laughed.

I asked my friend Andrew what he would do for a First.

"Hmmm. I don't know."

Cleo's mom, Brooke, couldn't think of anything either.

Cleo, however, announced, "I'm going to try new things too." We high-fived.

It wasn't by chance that the child among us was the one who immediately understood and liked the idea of "Firsts." As children, our lives are full of Firsts: first taste of ice cream, first time riding a bike, first day of school. We're like sponges. We want to try everything. We can't wait for new experiences.

As we get older there's still so much that's fresh, new, and exciting: first kiss, first driver's license, first heartbreak, first job, first plane ride. Those experiences shape you, stretch you, and bring new wonder to life.

But at some point, the Firsts in life dry up. You get busy with school, work, family, kids, and responsibilities. You get locked into your routines. You get comfortable. You go to the same places, have the same friends, do the same job, eat the same things. Then one day, you wake up and realize that the spontaneity and adventure are gone. You're living in *Groundhog Day*. You know that something needs to change, but change is scary. So you wait and nothing changes. You're stuck.

Before I started my Year of Firsts, I was stuck.

From the outside, my life at age fifty-three looked fine. I had a good job. I had plenty of accomplishments as a journalist. My marriage of twenty-five-plus years was stable. Physically, there was nothing wrong. And yet in 2009 everything was wrong. I felt lost, angry, and frustrated.

The economy was tanking. My job as an investigative reporter at a local television station in Philadelphia was changing. Friends I loved were moving. Longtime coworkers were leaving. Reporting resources were shrinking. Budgets were being cut. I resented the new technology and social media I was being asked to embrace at work. "I don't text!" I would snarl. "Facebook is for morons."

I stubbornly tried to do things the way I'd always done them, but I felt like I was beating my head against a wall. It was exhausting. For the first time in my life I felt old and out of touch.

Worst of all, I didn't like this version of myself. I had survived having my entire large intestine removed when I was thirty-three. I had survived breast cancer at thirty-five. I survived kidney cancer at age forty-five. I should have been dancing every day like Gene Kelly in *Singing in the Rain* just to be breathing, right? But I wasn't.

Perhaps it was because I had survived all of that that I was even more distressed. Days, weeks, and months were going by and I wasn't appreciating and enjoying them. I didn't want to get out of bed. I also knew being stressed and unhappy for that long wasn't good for my head or my health. And I didn't have time to move to Italy to go find myself, or meditate on my navel in Bali. Still, something had to give: I had to figure out how to get unstuck.

My smart, tech-savvy twenty-three-year-old daughter was worried about me. She hadn't really seen me like this before. She pushed me.

"Maybe you need a new creative outlet," Alexa suggested.

"Maybe," I said.

"Maybe you should start a blog." Now, she was bugging me.

"What the hell is a blog?"

"An online journal. You can write about anything."

It just sounded like more work to me. And I had no idea what I'd write about. I couldn't think of just one thing that would keep my interest. Still, for some reason I mulled it over. Maybe my daughter was right, I thought. Maybe I could blog. Maybe I could write about doing a lot of new things.

"What if I try something new every week? I'll write about that."

My daughter was having none of it. "No, something new every day!"

Now there was a crazy idea.

"Start making a list of things you've never done," she said. "They don't have to be big things like skydiving. Instead, don't swear for a day. Eat vegetarian for a day. Stuff like that."

There it was. The idea scared and excited me at the same time. I knew that was a good sign. Just like that, my Year of Firsts was born.

And that's how I found myself running into the freezing ocean at full speed on New Year's Day 2010. Surprise—it turns out that there's a perfectly good reason that sane people do something as insane as the Polar Bear Plunge: It's exhilarating! It's a full-on slap-in-the-face wake-up call. I ran out of the water soaked, shaken, and proud. It was the first of 365 Firsts.

For every day that year, I did something that I had never done before and blogged about it at luanncahn.com. When I could, I captured each First on video in all its goofy, seat-of-my-pants glory. I also established a few ground rules:

◇ A First could be something I hadn't tried in ten years. If you did your last cartwheel at nine, doing one at fifty-three counts as a first, believe me.

◇ No risking my life bungee jumping. I jumped out of a plane when I was twenty-one. I felt no need to sign forms that stated no one would be responsible in the "event of my death."

◇ My schedule was absolutely nuts, so I gave myself permission to embrace whatever small Firsts came my way in the course of a 24/7 life.

◇ No cheating. I couldn't skip a day. I had to do a First and document it.

My daughter was wrong; it wasn't easy to find a First every day. But she was also right. I needed this. I'd forgotten how much fun it is to try something new. It didn't take much time before I was excited to get up every morning. I knew that I was going to do something that day for the very first time.

What did I learn? Firsts are the antidote for being stuck.

My Firsts ranged from riding a mechanical bull to rapelling into an underground cave. I spoke to a complete stranger on the street. I smoked my first cigar. I shoveled horse manure. I learned to surf. I took a drum lesson from a famous '80s rocker. I spent time in a wheelchair. I attempted to experience blindness. I ate dessert for an entire day (I do not recommend this).

Some Firsts were pivotal moments, like going back to school. Many Firsts were just what I could find on the fly, like walking my dog Angel backwards one day. Some were painful parts of real life, like the day I had to put Angel to sleep. And still others were whatever I could work into my crazy-busy schedule as a journalist, TV personality, speaker, wife, and mom.

No, I didn't join the Peace Corps or run with the bulls in Pamplona. But, as I discovered during the year, it's the smallest changes that eventually change everything: They got me "unstuck." They brought the life back into my life. And they also made me realize something incredibly important: Firsts don't have to be big, dramatic, and risky to recharge and reinvent your life. By just trying small things, you begin to see the world around you with fresh, child's eyes. Doing Firsts retrains us, takes what might seem predictable and smothering, and transforms it into something filled with learning, fun, and possibility.

Word of my Year of Firsts experience quickly grew online. More than eighty thousand people watched my videos on YouTube and I was able to share with thousands of others through NBC 10 (where I worked), Facebook, and Twitter. Dozens of viewers and fans offered ideas, lessons, suggestions, and support to "Keep going!," and some even invited me to come share a First experience with them!

But one of the most exciting things that happened was that people didn't just watch me do Firsts—they started doing them too. And this is why I wrote *I Dare Me.*

My hope is *I Dare Me* dares you! I want you to look at your world with new eyes, to make your own list of Firsts, to stop waiting for someone to rescue you from whatever you can't control and to rescue yourself with something new every day. That's how your life starts to change, one First at a time.

I've divided the book into ten chapters to tell you stories about the different kinds of Firsts I tried and to give you ideas on how to launch your own Year of Firsts. You can start anywhere in the book, whether it's the beginning, or flipping through and finding something that jumps out at you.

Because I'm a journalist and a sometime-skeptic when I hear about books that will "change your life," I've included scientific information and studies in each chapter that show how First experiences can be positive and even life altering. Though my own experience is anecdotal, you'll read about how new experiences can change your fears, brain, and heart, and put you on a better path in your life.

If you'd like to see what some of these Firsts actually look like, visit my blog, luanncahn.com. You'll also find stories of other people's Firsts, and you can share your First adventures too.

I know what it's like to be stuck. I know what it's like to feel sad and think you have lost the ability to change whatever situation you are in. But I promise you, change starts with doing something new, something different from what you did yesterday.

I grew. I changed. My world opened up and is still evolving today as a result of my Year of Firsts. It's my greatest hope that you find a similar spark somewhere in these pages, something that lights a fire under you to make this not just a life, but your best life. I dare you. I double dare you.

CHAPTER 1

Running with Strangers in Speedos

Firsts That Overcome Fears

We don't always know where our fears come from, but I remember quite vividly the day I decided I was afraid of the ocean.

I was about eight years old when my father took our family on a business trip to Jekyll Island, Georgia. I'd never seen the ocean before, and I was so excited. A storm was blowing in, but I begged my father to let me go into the water. He hesitated, but I insisted.

My father took my small hand and I felt completely safe as we waded into the pounding surf. My dad lifted me with one arm over a wave so it wouldn't hit me then put me back in the water then lifted me again, and I laughed so hard I could barely catch my breath. "More, more!" I yelled, wanting to go out farther. But he must have sensed we had pushed the limits of safety on this little adventure. Rain was coming down. He turned us around to head back to shore.

As we waded in, a big unexpected wave smashed down on both of us from behind. I felt my hand slip from my father's grip. I was rolling under the wave like I was in a washing machine. I couldn't breathe, couldn't get to the surface. I was swallowing water. In the seconds before I felt my dad's meaty hand reach into the water and pull me up like a drowned pup, I felt sheer terror.

On shore I sobbed and choked up seawater while my dad patted me on the back and tried to reassure me I was okay. "You're fine, all right? You're okay. You just swallowed a little water."

But I was shaken to the core. My mom scolded my father for taking me out in the rough surf. Despite coaxing the next day from him, I stubbornly refused to go back into the water. The waves that had so excited and thrilled me at first had whipped my behind and left me coughing up on the sand. Nope, at eight years old, I decided I didn't like waves anymore. And throughout adulthood, I held on to that irrational fear.

Of course there are rational fears in life. Fear of jumping out of a plane? Sure. Bungee jumping? Absolutely.

But some fears prevent you from enjoying life.

Until my Year of Firsts I hadn't thought much about my fear of the ocean. It was just something I accepted, even though my family vacations on St. Augustine beach in Florida every year. My husband is from that area. I had grown very used to watching him, all of his siblings, and our daughter swim far out into the ocean, boogie boarding and body surfing while I sat on the shore. They always looked like they were having so much fun. I'd feel a tug of envy that I didn't get to share that part of our vacation experience together, but I held back. Sometimes I would wade in up to my knees, but I quickly turned around, my inner eight-year-old reminding me the waves were not to be trusted. I knew I was missing out, but I just didn't want to deal with it.

I suppose that's why it surprised the heck out of my family when I told them I was going to start my Year of Firsts with a Polar Bear Plunge. My husband, Phil, laughed, "You don't go out in the ocean in the middle of summer. You're going to go into the ocean in the middle of winter?"

I knew it sounded crazy. It made no sense, and yet it made perfect sense. I'd spent all these years standing on the edge of the ocean. Was it just one of the many ways I was standing on the edge of my life? The idea of facing a fear, starting a year of new experiences, and the Polar Bear Plunge all converged in my brain at the same time. My gut told me it was coming together like this for a reason. This was exactly the right place to begin.

And that's how I ended up, on New Year's Day 2010 at age fifty-three, standing on the edge of the Atlantic Ocean.

I'm sure you've heard of Polar Bear Plunges. That's when otherwise normal people run into the freezing ocean or jump into an icy lake to mark the beginning of a New Year. I watched the news clips every year like almost everyone else, thinking the same thing: *Those people are nuts! Why would any normal person risk frostbite on body parts that should never be frostbitten?*

And yet, there I was in my bathing suit and gym shorts, terrified and nauseous, getting ready to take "the plunge."

It was my first "First"; a big mental hurdle First. It was a First so far outside of my comfort zone that my inner eight-year-old was pleading with me: *Please, let's go home. I hate waves. I hate cold. Why are we here?*

Everything in my being wanted to listen to the child that had been rolled in the ocean so long ago. But knowing the little scaredy-cat might show up, I brought reinforcements. My twenty-three-year-old daughter, Alexa, was by my side with a flip cam, a change of clothes, and a bucket of moral support.

"Mom, do you have any last words?"

"Yeah, call 9-1-1 if I need it!"

A TV news crew from my station was on hand ready to capture my plunge for posterity. And since I'd told absolutely everyone I was going to do this (friends, family, coworkers, and vague acquaintances), I didn't have any wiggle room to weasel out.

Thank goodness other veteran plungers that gathered were only too happy to have a first-timer in their midst. They offered words of encouragement.

"You'll feel warmer when you get out."

"Don't go into the ocean with the only dry pair of socks you have."

"It doesn't count if your head doesn't go under the water."

My head has to go under the water?

Images of my little eight-year-old body unable to get a breath, swirling in the ocean made me queasy.

We lined up on the shore, waiting for the signal to run.

I felt frozen, literally and figuratively. I had no faith that my feet would voluntarily move on their own and hurl my body and head into the ocean. I was going to need some help.

I asked the strangers in Speedos next to me to please grab my hands and just drag me into the water if necessary. They were more than happy to oblige.

I tried to push a whole host of fears aside as I dug my toes into the sand sans socks: fear of putting my head in the ocean, fear of looking foolish, fear my bathing suit and gym shorts would ride up and expose my pale butt, fear of not following through with what I'd told everyone I was going to do, fear this might be the stupidest and most humiliating thing I'd ever tried, and of course my childhood fear that the ocean would just swallow me up whole and I'd never surface again. Yet in spite of those fears, there was also this other voice inside of me urging me on. It was time to swim, leave the shore, join hands with people I didn't know; a first step toward joining my own family in the St. Augustine waves. I thought, *Push forward. This is right. This is crazy right. I dare me.*

The horn went off, and good to their word, my strangers, now heroes in Speedos, pulled me into the ocean. My feet moved. I was actually running forward!

The next thing I knew . . . SPLAT! Facedown into the surf. Head under water. My knee scraped on the sand. The whole thing happened in seconds. I heard a voice yell, "YOU DID IT!" And then I felt a hand reach down and grab me, much the way my father grabbed me up out of the ocean as a child. I was screaming my lungs out like a victorious lunatic warrior running up onto the sand, hand in hand with one of my new Speedo friends.

Even now, my heart beats faster just reliving that moment in my mind. I was so happy, laughing, exhilarated. My daughter danced around me as I triumphantly wrapped myself in a towel feeling like I'd just won a gold medal. And here's something crazy. I did feel warm standing there sopping wet on the beach. I was warm!

I babbled breathlessly in front of the camera and finally said, "I really needed to start this year with a splash and I couldn't think of anything bigger than this." I proudly pulled on my I Survived the Polar Bear Plunge T-shirt. And I understood. Polar Bear Plungers aren't crazy. (Okay, maybe a little.) They just want to remind themselves they are on this planet living full-out, passionate lives, kicking fear in the face. Now, I was one of them.

Conquering the Polar Bear Plunge gave me the courage to go back into the ocean. I later went surfing during my Year of Firsts. Yes, I got bonked in the head with the board, negotiated waves that scared me, and the whole time, I kept an eye out for man-eating sharks. But I kind of stood up on that surfboard, gave my family a great laugh, and proved to myself again, I was stronger and braver than I'd thought.

It turns out the edge of the ocean was just the beginning; a jumping-off point for an adventure that would change everything.

Think about the limits that fear and insecurities have put on your own life.

Maybe you never learned to swim and you're afraid to jump in the pool. Maybe you are terrified of public speaking and you want to give a toast at a wedding. Perhaps you have held back from making amends with a relative or have apprehension about going back to school. There's no doubt these first experiences dealing with facing a fear are the toughest and the most symbolic. In my mind, they are also the most rewarding.

Firsts like singing in public or going to the movies by yourself may seem like silly fears to conquer on the surface. I can assure you, it's more than that. Facing and getting beyond any fear demonstrates in a memorable way that you can take a risk and not only survive, but feel more alive. If it's an obstacle for you, then overcoming it will give you an incredible life high.

As I took on unnerving challenges during my Year of Firsts, I discovered it only reinforced my confidence to keep going. It taught me that some risks and experiences are just worth it, no matter how fearful you might be. Otherwise, fear's just a prison that keeps us from living the life we really want, isn't it?

Your journey facing a fear must be meaningful and unique to you. Only you know the first step you should take. For me it was finally, purposefully stepping off the sand, symbolically plunging into the water with a public, flying leap. I let the waves hit me again and allowed myself to laugh at the childhood fear that I'd held on to for far too long.

You may share some of the fears I tried to tackle: going a day without looking in the mirror, talking to a stranger, or finding out what it might be like to be confined to a wheelchair. These Firsts altered my view of the world and myself a little. I promise, whatever fears you decide to face, facing them will allow you to see yourself differently. Others will see you in a different light too. And that will just be the beginning of your new and reinvigorated life.

A Day Without a Mirror: Day 3

When you are through changing, you are through.
—BRUCE BARTON

In some ways I failed miserably at this First. It's difficult to completely avoid all mirrors for a whole day.

I had no idea how often I looked in the mirror until I tried

SOME SCIENTIFIC EVIDENCE TO INSPIRE YOU TO FACE YOUR FEARS

- A UCLA study found that mice can be conditioned to be afraid of "white noise" with an electric shock. It also found the fear could be eliminated by exposing the same mice repeatedly to the "white noise" without the shock. Researchers believe results have human applications. Makes sense. Fear of flying? Fly more.

- Some research suggests getting fit will help fight fear and anxiety. One Princeton University study shows rats who exercise grow neurons in their brains that are less responsive to cortisol, a stress hormone. (I know, more rodent research.)

- Studies show remembering courageous acts from our past can help us find the courage needed to face a new fear or challenge.

not to: an entire hour getting ready to leave the house, the whole time I'm at the gym, the makeup compact mirror checks, the bathroom mirror checks, the I'm-not-really-checking-myself-out mirror checks.

In the morning, I succeeded in avoiding the mirror in my bathroom when brushing my teeth and hair. Putting my contacts in was tricky but doable. Makeup? Minimal; just some lip gloss, some tinted moisturizer. I risked putting on mascara. Who knows if it smudged? Vanity, I guess, made me take a chance.

I went to the gym and forgot there were mirrors everywhere. Treadmill? Oops. Weight room? There I am again.

I met my friend Loraine for coffee and told her about my First that day. . . . I had to ask, "So, do I look okay?"

She laughed. "Yes, you're fine. Why are you doing this?"

"Because," I said, "I think I worry too much about what I look like. I want to see if I can free myself of mirrors and my fear of not looking okay."

Loraine said, "I'm your mirror and I say you look okay."

"Okay."

I ran errands, came home, made dinner, consciously avoiding bathroom mirrors.

For some reason, going without mirrors made me think about when I was twelve and went to overnight camp. My ten bunkmates and I would fight for time in front of the one full-length mirror in the cabin. I was prissy then and hated the sleepovers we had in the woods. But I also remember it was a relief even at that age, when we girls left the mirror and coed activities and camped out by ourselves.

In the cabin, we could be incredibly mean and critical of each other. In the woods, it was different. It was acceptable to be grimy and dirty. No one cared or judged the way you looked.

I never learned to light a fire with one match (that'd be a good First). I hated sleeping on the ground. But, in the woods with no mirrors, we got outside of our petty selves. We weren't fighting over the hair dryer. Around the campfire we talked about what we wanted to be when we grew up.

A day without a mirror is kind of like a day in the woods. I was fine walking around without a lot of makeup.

Okay, a good night's sleep and a little lipstick never hurt. But in the end, of course, who we see in the mirror is mostly a reflection of how we feel about ourselves. And, I was reminded by this First, you don't really need a mirror for that.

Other Firsts Like This to Try

◇ Go a day without makeup.

◇ Plan a First camping trip.

◇ Have a wear-your-pajamas-everywhere day.

Talk to a Stranger: Day 16

Fear makes strangers of people who would be friends.
—SHIRLEY MACLAINE

As a reporter, I've spent my life walking up to strangers and starting conversations. Okay, there was a camera person with me and I had a microphone. Still, how different could this be? Let me tell you, it's more challenging than you might imagine.

I decided to try this First at Philadelphia's Rittenhouse Square. It's a city park right in the middle of some of the ritziest real estate in town. There's shopping and outdoor cafes on the edges of the park.

On a nice day, it draws one of the most diverse and eclectic crowds you could possibly put together. There are artists with easels sketching the park fountain. There are college students playing music. There are young couples with babies stretched out on the grass. Business executives in suits sit on benches eating lunch or reading the paper. There are millionaires sharing benches with homeless people. Sometimes it's difficult to tell who is who.

That day, I walked through the park looking for someone I could approach. I don't know if I made people feel uncomfortable, but no one would make eye contact with me. Everyone seemed to be preoccupied all of a sudden; engaged in conversation or engrossed in a book. I walked up and down the main path through the park. Finally, I spotted someone.

He was an older gentleman, African American, looking a bit disheveled with some shopping bags at his feet. I couldn't find anyone who looked more different from me.

I thought he might be homeless. I wasn't sure.

He was sitting on a bench by himself staring out into space. I realized I felt nervous contemplating sitting down next to him. What if he was a whacko? What if he didn't want to talk to me? I felt self-conscious, and walked by him several times before I just willed myself to make my move and plop down next to him.

"Hi, nice day, isn't it?"

What else was I going to say? To my surprise, his whole expression changed. He smiled real big.

"Sure is."

That's how we started.

He told me his name was Jim. I asked if he came to the park often. He said he did, ever since his wife, Trisha, died. He told me they were married for twenty-eight years and that he lived nearby. Within minutes of talking I realized he was far from homeless, but he was clearly lonely and in some way lost.

Jim told me he had been an investment banker and his wife had had her own business.

They'd traveled the world together. He said, "I miss her. I miss her every day." He quoted a line from a poem she left him before she died. "Don't promise me forever. Love me today."

"You mind me asking? What happened to her? How did she die?"

"She died of breast cancer."

My heart went out to him. I knew in that moment, we were really not so different as I had first imagined.

"I'm so sorry for your loss. I'm a breast cancer survivor. I was diagnosed with cancer when I was thirty-five."

Jim looked at me like he didn't believe me at first. Then he looked away and told me more about his life with Trisha. He asked me a couple of times, "What made you talk to me?"

I said, "I just woke up this morning and decided I was going to talk to someone I never talked to before."

He laughed, but asked again, "Why me?"

I just said, "I don't know. I guess I liked your face, your friendly face."

That wasn't exactly the truth, but he looked at me like I was an angel that had been sent from heaven. I'd broken the silence. For a few minutes he wasn't alone.

I'd been so caught up in our conversation I forgot to take some video for my blog. I asked if I could record him a little in the end. I wanted to know if I would see him again and where he usually sits. He told me he comes more often when it's warm.

Every time I walk through the park at Rittenhouse Square I look for Jim, but I've never seen him since our one chance meeting. If I didn't have the video, I might start to wonder if he had been an angel sent there for me. But he was very real and very sad. Yet, I knew our little interaction made both of our days better.

Call it karma. Call it whatever you want. It felt like that conversation was supposed to happen. It reminds me we are all so much more alike than we acknowledge. That if you listen, you will find some common ground, and it is usually our fears and flawed initial judgments that keep us from saying "hello."

Talk to a stranger today. See what happens.

Other Firsts Like This to Try

◊ Introduce yourself and chat with the neighbor you only wave at.

◊ Go to a party and strike up a conversation with someone you've never met before.

◊ Buy coffee for the stranger standing in line behind you.

Go to the Movies by Myself: Day 30

You block your dream when you allow your fear to grow bigger than your faith.
—MARY MANIN MORRISSEY

"Ticket for one?" I asked almost like I was questioning, *Is this allowed?*

The guy in the ticket booth gave me the evil eye as I took

my flip cam out to document my First for the day. Hard to believe a grown woman, who is fairly well traveled, has interviewed celebrities and presidents, and went on TV for a living never had the guts to go to the movies by herself before. This, I swear, was the case.

My ticket was for a 1:00 weekend matinee, and I was glad there was no line. It was silly, but I wasn't sure I really wanted anyone I knew to see me, or for that matter, anyone I didn't know.

It was a month into doing new things daily. That week I'd been fencing, walking for miles in the woods, and trying an experimental dance class in addition to my regular crazy work schedule. I was beat. The idea of just sitting on my derriere in a movie theater sounded wonderful.

Still, I was self-conscious about this First. What would people think? *No friends? Poor dear alone with her big bucket of popcorn?*

I don't know where I got the idea you can't go to the movies alone, but I feel like it was ingrained in my things-girls-just-don't-do brain. I love going to the movies, yet if someone couldn't go with me, I'd of course wait for some other time. Why? Why do we let fear of some weird social judgment stop us from doing something we want to do?

Even my husband seemed concerned as I headed out the door.

"Why can't I come with you?"

"It's a First. Don't worry. I promise I'll be home alive in a couple of hours."

Once I had my ticket, I went right to the popcorn counter. I didn't look anyone in the eye. I admit, for all my bravado, I was anxious to get into the dark theater and become invisible. I picked a seat toward the back. I looked around a little before the lights dimmed. There were a few other people seated by themselves. I felt better.

I dug into my popcorn as the lights went down and the previews started.

I felt proud of myself. What had I feared?

The movie, *Extraordinary Measures* with Harrison Ford, was mostly forgettable. I can't even tell you what it was about.

But the experience of getting past my fear of going alone, as easy as it was in reality, made me feel, well . . . happy. I walked out smiling. I even acknowledged the other theatergoers. "Hi, how ya doing? Awful movie, wasn't it?"

I enjoyed my own company, not sharing the popcorn.

I can tell you, doing this First actually cured me. I have no problem taking myself to the movies now. And conquering this small fear gave me the confidence to go it alone for many other fabulous Firsts during the year.

Your own company is good enough. Take yourself somewhere wonderful, relax and enjoy.

Other Firsts Like This to Try

◊ Eat at a fancy restaurant by yourself.

◊ Go to a party by yourself.

◊ Take a day trip or a vacation by yourself.

Sing in Front of a Crowd: Day 122

Many of our fears are tissue-paper-thin, and a single courageous step would carry us clear through them.

—BRENDAN FRANCIS

As a child, I was sure I was the next Barbra Streisand. I'd step up on the stone bench next to the fireplace in our living room like it was a stage, hold my fake microphone, and belt out "Don't Rain on My Parade" for thousands of invisible fans.

In elementary school, I sang in a choir. As a teen, I sang in some musicals. In college I did a little singing for skits. I even sang in front of Bill and Hillary Clinton in a political musical spoof called the Farkleberry Follies in Little Rock, Arkansas. Clinton was governor and I was a young twenty-three-year-old reporter (NO! nothing happened). The Clintons sat in the front row, laughed, and applauded as I tried to mimic one of the governor's female staffers.

As far as I can recall that's the last time I sang publicly. Why? I guess the same reason many of us stop doing lots of things we did in our youth. I was loud and generally on key but never a great singer. I knew that. So I let go of my fantasy Barbra Streisand act and moved on to more serious aspirations in my adult life. I limited singing out loud to the car, when I was driving alone.

Thirty years after my last singing act in Little Rock, someone suggested I sing publicly for a First. My heart leaped. Oh, that would be fun, but would I completely embarrass myself? I knew it would be a challenging First, and I wasn't ready. I tucked the idea away and didn't think about it for months.

By May in my Year of Firsts, it was a challenge just to come up with something new every day. Ideas I'd passed over once as impossible or improbable or too difficult stared at me from my list. I was learning not to eliminate any idea no matter how unlikely. I found the more I pushed myself out of my comfort zone, the more rewarding and interesting the experience was.

I was making plans to emcee the annual Renaissance Ball for the Crohn's and Colitis Foundation in Philadelphia and realized my best opportunity for a good First that day would be in front of the crowd of five hundred. I looked at my list. *Sing in public? Hmmm. There's a live band at the ball. Now or never.*

I have a special relationship with the Philadelphia Chapter of the Crohn's and Colitis Foundation of America. Two years before I was diagnosed with breast cancer I was diagnosed with ulcerative colitis, an intestinal bowel disorder. The disease runs in my family, so it wasn't a huge surprise when at the age of thirty-three I was in so much pain I couldn't eat, sleep, or work. I needed surgery. I spent months in the hospital before doctors concluded my entire large intestine would have to be removed.

It was terrifying to face that reality. But my family and the CCFA helped me get through months of recovery and adjustment. In the end, the surgery allowed me to live again and go back to doing all the things I loved. I owed CCFA a debt of gratitude, and as a thank-you, I hosted their annual ball every year.

Thinking about the real fear of getting through that surgery put my fear of singing in front of a crowd in perspective. I could handle this.

The CCFA agreed to let me auction off a song to the highest bidder. Whoever offered the most money to send kids with Crohn's or colitis to a special camp could pick the song I would sing.

I felt pretty good about my decision until the time came to do it. All of a sudden, I was nervous, palms sweating. What if I sounded like a frog? What if someone picked a song I didn't know? What if I completely embarrassed myself, and, even worse, what if no one wanted to bid on me singing a song?

I was relieved when a few people I knew in the crowd raised their hands to bid. One possible humiliation bypassed. Sue and Gene Kestenbaum generously offered to pay for three kids to go to camp and won the "auction" without knowing what they were in for with their "prize." They are brave, sweet people.

Sue gamely came up with the song "You Made Me Love You." I kind of remembered the tune but I didn't know the words. I ran the request back to the band leader. He knew the song well, quickly scratched the words down on paper, and quietly sang the song for me so I could learn it. I only had a few minutes; the crowd was waiting.

I reminded myself that this was for charity. It didn't have to be perfect. Not the point.

I held the words of the song in front of me. The band started to play. I went to the podium microphone and started tentatively singing . . . "You made me love you, I didn't want to do it. . . ."

People kept eating and talking. No one but the Kestenbaums was really paying attention. No one was throwing tomatoes at me or booing either. All of a sudden, I felt braver. *See. It doesn't matter.*

That's when I decided "Barbra" was in the house. I picked up the wireless mic and my voice got stronger. I wasn't afraid anymore. I remembered I loved singing in campy shows.

I strutted across the ballroom floor toward the Kestenbaums. After all, they paid for this! "Give me, give me, give me, give me what I cry for . . ." I sang. Dramatically pointing toward the Kestenbaums, I delivered the big goofy finish: "You know you made me love youuuuuuuuuu!"

Clapping . . . YES!

I did it!

I admit I'm a bit disappointed I have not received one request for a repeat performance.

Yep, it was gutsy and it was corny. It wasn't *American Idol* material. But, I look at that video and feel rewarded every time. It's a reminder of who I am when I'm fearless and ready to expose my best, crazy, fully authentic self.

We all need those moments. We all need to know we can push past our fears to step on to whatever "stage" in life makes our heart beat faster. Pick a First that does just that, for you.

Other Firsts Like This to Try

◊ Try out for a community play.

◊ Speak up at a public meeting. Make a passionate speech from the heart.

◊ Start writing the book, the play, the song, the article you've been thinking about in your head.

Spend a Day in a Wheelchair: Day 208

The only disability in life is a bad attitude.
—SCOTT HAMILTON

When I was in my twenties, I had a young friend who was disabled. An accident put her in a wheelchair for life. She was an activist, pushing for accessibility, and she often reminded me I was just a "TAB," a temporarily able-bodied person. I didn't like to think about that idea, that at anytime I might experience an accident or illness that could make me permanently disabled, but I always remembered it.

I suppose that's why I resisted and in some way feared the idea of spending time in a wheelchair. I'm not a superstitious person, yet something about trying to pretend you're disabled felt like tempting fate.

But the MS Society in Philadelphia was persistent. The organization learned I was doing first-time experiences and they wanted a reporter to help publicize the twentieth anniversary of the Americans with Disabilities Act. They pitched: "What a great First! Put you in a wheelchair for a day."

"Isn't it insulting to people who really are confined to a wheelchair for me to fake a disability?" I asked.

The MS society assured me a day in a wheelchair was not an offensive gesture—quite the opposite. I had run out of objections.

Fred Schwartz kindly offered to be my guide along with an MS representative. He'd been in a wheelchair with MS for eight years, struck with the debilitating disease in the middle of his life. We met at the TV station, and he offered to let me borrow his lighter, smaller wheelchair for the experiment. He was assisted into a big clunky old heavy wheelchair we had in storage at the station. Fred showed me how to move myself forward and backwards and we were off.

The first half hour was a breeze. What had I been worried about? I rolled myself down the station hallways to the cafeteria like I was testing out a new toy. I was able to reach the coffee, take an elevator to the newsroom, and find ramps that gave me access to different levels of the floor. I got this. No problem.

I didn't meet any challenge until I actually tried to do some work, and then I found myself up against one obstacle after another. I never gave a second thought to the heavy doors throughout the station that swing shut. How do you hold a door for yourself and go through it in a wheelchair? You don't. You have to ask someone for help. Immediately, I felt some loss of control and independence. There was this sense of feeling like a child, as coworkers chatted at me from above.

Cables blocked my path in the studio. I couldn't maneuver in the news truck garage and there was no lift to get me in a van.

It wasn't long after I'd guzzled a couple cups of coffee that I was forced to give our accessible bathroom a road test too. I awkwardly rolled myself into the stall, which reminded me of parallel parking (something I'm really bad at). It was tricky going through the motions of getting myself out of the wheelchair onto the toilet seat, then back into the wheelchair. I called on every muscle I had to pull myself up and lower myself down with the aid of a stall handrail. Not fun.

But the most challenging and scariest part of the day was leaving the building. Fred led the way. My arms were giving out shortly after rolling out of the station and up a sidewalk with a slight incline. The worst was yet to come.

We tried to cross the four lanes of City Avenue to go shopping across the street. We waited for a light to turn green and I pushed my wheels as hard as I could to propel myself to the other side before the light turned red. I panicked, nearly tipping over from bumps and cracks in the pavement. A driver slammed on his horn, yelling, "Get out of the way!"

I wasn't moving fast enough. How could people be so mean? I felt small and threatened. I thought about how many disabled men and women in wheelchairs I'd seen crossing at this very same intersection over the years, coming from a nearby rehabilitation facility, trying to get to the shopping center. I'd never thought about the stamina and courage it took just to attempt a bit of independent living and freedom.

We never got to the shopping. Fred could see I was shaken. He took it in stride. He was used to this. He told me you gain confidence with practice just like anything else. I wanted to go back to the safety of the station.

In the end, I didn't spend a day in a wheelchair. It was just three eye-opening hours. I was relieved and grateful to get out of that wheelchair and assure myself that all was right in my world and this was just a test.

Fred hoisted himself back into the wheelchair I'd borrowed. He didn't say much. He didn't have to.

Whatever worries, deadlines, or problems I had that day suddenly seemed inconsequential. I always thought of myself as being sensitive to the needs of the disabled.

I felt ashamed. I didn't have a clue. The experience only

gave me the tiniest glimpse of what it would be like to try to navigate the world from a wheelchair, and I had a hard time handling it.

I now understood why the MS Society wanted me to live this First. For days, I had new eyes. I'd walk into a room and think, *Could I get in here with a wheelchair?* I watched someone in a motorized chair at the grocery try to get to something beyond her reach. *Can I get that for you?*

Did I just not see before or did I just want to turn away from those who reminded me, as my friend did so long ago, I might be that person someday? I might just be a temporarily able-bodied person.

I like to think my vision has permanently changed, but our brains have a way of returning us to a place where we feel safe. It takes some effort to try to experience something you never want to happen to you and then keep that memory in the forefront of your mind. As tough as it was, I wish this First was somehow a requirement for everyone. I have no doubt it would make the world a kinder and more accessible place.

Other Firsts Like This to Try

◇ Spend time blindfolded.

◇ Block your sense of hearing with noise-canceling headphones.

◇ Ask a friend with a disability to help you experience what they experience even if it's just for a few hours.

Final Thoughts

What are you waiting for? Don't let fear of failure or rejection deter you. In your own heart you know what you want to do. You know you may be missing opportunities and fun and love in your life because facing a fear seems too risky, too uncomfortable. These Firsts are an opportunity to stretch your limits, to go where you are afraid to go. Face these fears and know they will help you get unstuck and propel you forward in your life.

Make a list of your smallest and biggest fears. Then take a leap of faith in yourself, your best self, and take them on one by one.

TIPS FOR FINDING FIRSTS THAT OVERCOME FEARS

- You might have the life equivalent of stage fright during the days and hours before you finally take on your fear. That's totally normal. Don't let it stop you.

- Try to stay in the moment of your First. Don't fret about what others might think. Who cares? This is your journey and your time.

- Record your First. Whether it's a picture or video, blog, or journal doesn't matter. Make sure you find a way to keep the memory. You can look back on it when you need inspiration for another challenge or just to enjoy a good laugh. You will always have it to remember your most courageous self.

- Bring moral support. You don't have to do this alone (unless the fear is doing something alone). Let friends and family lift you up and help you on your journey. It's okay to ask for help.

- Partner up. Maybe there is someone else who is facing the same fear and wants to try a first with you. Then you can celebrate your success together.

- Pay attention to that feeling of fear and excitement at the same time. It's a sign you are doing exactly the First you should be doing.

- Tell everyone you know what you are about to attempt. You are more likely to follow through. Your friends will hold you to it.

CHAPTER 2

I Got a New "Ad-dee-tood"

Firsts for Busy People

In some parts of Philly, the word isn't "attitude," it's "ad-dee-tood." Picture Rocky saying it: "Yo, Adrian. I got a new byou-dee-ful ad-dee-tood!"

Six months into my Year of Firsts, I felt a little like Rocky. I was the scrappy underdog fighting back with my "new ad-dee-tood self."

I knew my life was changing because I didn't wake up angry anymore. I was jumping out of bed—no time to linger. Every day, I was having fun, and my curious friends and coworkers wanted to know what I was up to:

"What's your First today?"

"I'm going to run the bases at the Phillies ballpark."

"Ooooh. Cool."

People began to look at me a little differently. Okay sure. They thought I'd gone a little around the bend. Maybe I had.

What I know is this: I didn't feel stuck. I was exploring any and all possibilities around me.

One day at the station, an email went out asking if anyone wanted to fill in cohosting our lifestyle and entertainment show in front of a studio audience, the *10! Show*. Sounded like a perfect First, so I volunteered. It was a hoot. I talked about My Year of Firsts and all the new things I'd been trying. I thought, *Well, that was a fun onetime gig.* But then they asked me back to do it again. Within a few months the executive producer wanted to know if I'd be willing to cohost the show full-time.

I was surprised someone was considering me for a completely different "out of the box" kind of role. I'd been an investigative reporter for the last ten years of my career, spending my days chasing down fraud and scams. Now, I was being asked if I wanted to interview actors like Bradley Cooper and cook with chefs like Paula Deen. It would be quite a career switch up.

Some of my friends questioned the wisdom of the move. My boss, understandably, had to be convinced it was something worth trying. But against plenty of advice to do otherwise, I pushed for it. In the spirit of my Year of Firsts I thought: *Go with it. This is all part of this crazy unpredictable journey. Who knows what it will lead to next? Good or bad, it sure won't be the same.*

Just as I started hosting the *10! Show*, another opportunity came along. I was asked if I would teach a graduate school investigative journalism class at Drexel University. I had always wanted to teach, and I knew this would be a perfect way to share and keep my hand in something I loved (investigative reporting) while trying something new.

I didn't think it was just a coincidence that more doors were opening. Since starting my Year of Firsts, I was beginning to show a new face to the world. Instead of being confused and resentful, I was full of hope and energy again. Those around me saw a new me with my new "ad-dee-tood."

However, as I jumped into all of these extra adventures, there was one problem: I was running around at a hundred miles an hour with my hair on fire. I was learning how to host and prepare for an hour-long show every day; I was prepping, reading, and grading for the class I taught every week; and I was doing Firsts and blogging every single day. Something had to change.

I wasn't about to quit doing Firsts. I knew they were the key to bringing freshness and vitality into my life. I just had to figure out a way to keep a lot of my Firsts during my workweek quick and easy.

I decided to make a list of Firsts that I could fit into my hectic days. I wrote down simple things like *taste every flavor at the ice cream store*. I'd always wanted an excuse to do that. Easy, right?

I came up with dozens of Firsts that could be done in no time. It took me five minutes to teach my dog how to high-five (okay, she was really smart). Ten minutes was all it took for me to learn to do a table trick with a salt shaker. Planting an herb garden? Fifteen short minutes!

Silly, right? But not really. These little Firsts added shots of joy and deliciousness to my life. They made each day a little more interesting. They got my brain buzzing with the energy of doing something new.

I found that being good at recognizing easy little Firsts meant being open-minded. One day I was working on a story about a horse stable, and while I was there, the family that owned the barn told me they were about to start mucking the stalls. "What's mucking?" I asked. "Oh," Patricia Cianflone said with a wink and a mischievous Tom Sawyer smile, "it's fun. Want to try?" "Sure. It will be a First." I had no idea "mucking" was removing dirty hay and horse manure! It was a first-time experience all right, and I'd worked it right into my day.

Wherever you spend a lot of time is a good place to look for easy Firsts. I could always find something at the gym. Someone's starting a new yoga wall class? I'm in. My husband plays racquetball. I asked him to show me how to play. Easy Firsts didn't take a big commitment, just the willingness to give it a go. My daughter taught me how to twirl a pen. Kitchen dancing was a cinch while making dinner.

Trying a new food was another easy First. An all "raw" meal? Chocolate-covered grasshoppers? I didn't have to like it. Just try it. At the very least the experience was a good story to tell.

Sometimes the easiest First was just a change in . . . say it . . . ad-dee-tood. I tried a no cursing day and a no whining day. I tried smiling all day. (Yes, fake it. There is scientific evidence it will make you feel better.) Granted, these Firsts may not have pushed me waaaay out of my comfort zone, but even just trying a new recipe presented a little risk, a little effort, a dash of spice in my life.

I make no apology for the simplicity of these things. Once you start incorporating Firsts into your life, you realize the small things do matter and help determine if you're going to have another *blah, done that before day*, or a day that leaves you energized and refreshed.

SCIENTIFIC EVIDENCE SMALL,
EASY CHANGES MAKE A DIFFERENCE

- Ad-dee-tood adjustment: just smile. Researchers at the University of California, Berkeley found that people who smile fully with their eyes and mouth were more likely to have a happier life. Numerous other studies show even faking a smile will not only make you happier, but will encourage others to mimic you and feel happier too.

- It's easy to grow happiness. Many studies suggest creating the simplest container herb or flower garden can improve your mood and reduce stress. One survey by professors at the Texas State University and Texas A&M found that gardeners report much more "zest for life" than non-gardeners.

- Do an easy First with your significant other. Researcher Arthur Aaron at State University of New York found that couples that did something new together were much more satisfied and happier than couples that did an activity they'd done many times before. So shake it up.

- Variety really is the spice of life. Psychologist Rich Walker of Winston-Salem State University reviewed thousands of event memories and diaries. He found people who participated in a variety of experiences held on to more positive emotions and minimized negative ones.

But most importantly, getting in the habit of doing easy little new things gets you used to taking risks, helps you see you can adapt and enjoy daily change. Look at easy Firsts as warm-up exercises, getting you primed and ready for the next big thing in your life.

A Day Without Cursing: Day 20

If you don't like something, change it. If you can't change it, change your attitude.
—MAYA ANGELOU

I have plenty of vices, but most aren't so obvious. I don't drink very often and I never smoke. But I do swear. A lot.

Most of my best swearing happens at work. Someone cancels an interview? *#$%!* Can't find something on my desk? (this happens often) *^%&*&^%$!* Technical difficulties? *$*^&*(@)#(&%)$Q!(&%)!*

I learned to swear at my first job in Chattanooga. I was twenty-one, fresh out of the University of Georgia's Journalism School, and the first full-time female reporter hired at WTVC in 1978. Some of the men in the newsroom weren't too happy about this. A few enjoyed finding the best way to torture me every day—testing for little chinks in my "oh, so very thin" armor at the time.

It only took my male coworkers a few days to realize I never cursed. They, of course, swore like sailors nonstop in the newsroom. This was in the good old days of smoking, drinking, sexual harassing, and fist fighting in TV newsrooms. (See the comedy version in the movie *Anchorman* with Will Ferrell.)

A conversation would go like this:

Hey, college girl, you ever say the word (&%^)!?*
Nope.
Why not? Just say it.

Silence.

Hey, ya'll, Lu Ann won't say (*&%^)!!

Juvenile, I know, but true. One day after being pushed to the limit by these guys, a string of curse words flew out of me in a rage. You'll have to use your imagination, but I used every expletive I'd never uttered before to tell them where to go. They roared with laughter. My face turned red, but they gave me a break after that.

This was my excuse for starting to curse. I collected an arsenal of words to fling out and strike anyone who even thought of messing with me.

Today, I curse for sport and, I suppose, unfortunately, out of thirty-plus years of habit. I have three favorite words. Two I use frequently without discretion. One, I keep in reserve when someone in my view has crossed some unforgivable line or everything has really gone to "you know what." I am capable of hiding this swearing habit from people who don't know me, but at work, the words fly.

My coworkers in Philadelphia had a good chuckle when I told them I was going to go a day without cursing for a First. Photographer Dave Bentley found it especially humorous: After working with me for eighteen years, he was quite used to my colorful vocabulary, and started counting the times I messed up.

"You do not have the ability to not use foul language throughout the day."

"I think I do."

"It's 10:24 a.m. You've already slipped twice."

"Really? Okay, they weren't bad ones."

He kept counting, laughing because I couldn't curse because I cursed.

Obviously this is an easy First to try. If you're like me, you just may not succeed. I did become acutely aware during the day that I curse much more than I thought. Dave lost count. I found I use my swear words like people use the word "like." Horrible. As the day went on, I had to literally stop before speaking out loud to edit myself; an interesting exercise.

I can't tell you this day changed my ways. It did not. I apparently like my little swears too much to let them go. But now I know. And I swear, I laughed a lot this day.

Other Firsts Like This to Try

◊ A day without coffee or gum or whatever you're addicted to.

◊ Don't say anything negative all day.

◊ Give out as many sincere compliments as you can all day.

Solo Kitchen Dancing: Day 57

Nobody cares if you can't dance well. Just get up and dance.
—DAVE BARRY

When my daughter, Alexa, was younger, sometimes while making dinner, she'd turn up some favorite song on the radio and we would "rock out" in the kitchen. Usually, this would result in fits of laughter as she watched her "old Mom" shake her bootie to Miley Cyrus's "See You Again" or Offspring's "Pretty Fly for a White Guy."

After Alexa grew up and moved to Los Angeles, I would come home after a long day of work and think about how I missed those times. I remember, no matter how bad the day was, we could always shake off all the negative energy, and sometimes, we'd end up rolling on the floor exhausted. There'd been no kitchen dancing, though, since she left home.

One particularly bitter February night when it felt like winter was squeezing the lifeblood out of me, I knew I had to change that. The house was empty. No one home but our dog, Angel. I turned on the radio and my flip cam to document my stunning solo kitchen dancing performance to "Roll It on Over." I shook it pretty good and felt better right away. I tried to get Angel to join me, but she just looked at me like I was some kind of wild woman. I put the video on YouTube and on my blog so that Alexa could see. It made her laugh.

When Mother's Day came along and we couldn't be together, Alexa surprised me with a different kind of "kitchen dancing." She called me up on Skype so we could see each other. She cranked up our favorite Miley Cyrus song, "See You Again," and we danced and laughed together despite all the miles between us.

It almost made me cry. It was easy, didn't cost a thing. A perfect gift. A First that touched my heart and the memories that connected us until I could really "see her again."

◊ Reach out to someone you haven't talked to since high school or college, and remember . . .

◊ Switch from your regular playlist, radio station, or music for a day. Listen to something different.

◊ Let off steam with a good primal scream. Record it.

Plant a Potted Herb Garden: Day 96

The greatest gift of the garden is the restoration of the five senses.
—HANNA RION

If you generally kill everything you plant, like I do, you might assume this First is not for you. But that's exactly why you *should* try it.

Every summer, I envy my friends who have lush vegetable gardens overflowing with tomatoes, squash, and peppers. I have been the appreciative recipient of beautiful fresh homegrown corn and zucchini. I've seen the love and care and time that go into those gardens.

Unfortunately, that's not me. I have trouble remembering to water a houseplant. But despite and because of my past, I was inspired to plant a potted herb garden for a First. I knew if somehow I managed to keep the herbs alive, I would actually use them. I went to a nursery and picked out sweet basil, Italian parsley, lemon thyme, and mint; threw them in a pot with soil, some water, left it outside in bright sun; and that was it. I think the whole thing took fifteen minutes tops.

At first, I was so excited to check on my little herbs. Every morning I'd run out to see if they were still kicking. I even watered them a little. Then, I forgot about them until I wanted to cook something.

But here's the surprising thing. Despite my utter and complete lack of care, I grew amazing sweet basil. I had enough basil for the neighborhood. The plant just took off. I gave fresh basil to anyone who came to the house. I could have bathed in my basil.

It gave me so much pleasure to step outside and pick a whole handful from my little container garden for a fresh pesto recipe. A tomato, mozzarella, and fresh basil salad? Delicious. Spaghetti sauce or tomato soup with fresh basil? Fabulous.

The other herbs? Well, I killed them. I guess they needed a little more care than the basil. The Italian parsley did hang in there for a while. Everything else just quickly withered and died.

But now, because of this First, I can tell you that I plant an herb container garden every year, and I'm still experimenting with herbs that can survive my "tough love" method of gardening. The basil always does well. If you can do just a little more tending than me (which wouldn't require much), you can probably enjoy growing thyme and mint and parsley too.

One day, I too will have an incredible garden and will pick my entire homemade fresh salad out of it. I look forward to that First. Until then, I'm building up my repertoire of basil recipes.

◊ Grow a container tomato plant. (I've actually done it. It's not that hard. Does require watering.)

◊ Grow container flowers. (Buy some hardy geraniums.) You can combine herbs and flowers in the same container.

◊ Try a Chia Pet. (Seriously.)

Taste 18 Flavors of Ice Cream: Day 250

I doubt whether the world holds for anyone a more soul-stirring surprise than the first adventure with ice cream.
—HEYWOOD BROUN

Sampling every ice cream flavor in the ice cream store has got to be my favorite easy First. There are, however, some things I should warn you about before you attempt this.

1. Not every ice cream parlor is going to think this is a great idea. I actually went to one where the owner said, "Only one taste for you!" Really? I left.

2. If you get to an ice cream parlor that has less than thirty-one flavors to try, that's okay. I tried eighteen flavors and two water ices and that was plenty.

3. Don't try this when the place is jam-packed. Go in the middle of a weekday when it's nice and quiet and the

employees are so bored they will be happy to see you and let you sample everything.

4. Ask for small samples. Believe me. They add up quick and you want to make it to the end of your ice cream sampling marathon without getting sick.

5. If you are going to blog or Facebook or tweet about your experience, tell the store manager. They may be even more enthusiastic about your taste test.

The young ladies manning the ice cream counter at the Carvel in Ardmore, Pennsylvania, were absolute gems. I was their only customer at the time I walked in, and they enjoyed announcing each flavor I sampled as if they were offering up a fine wine, or some divine gourmet cheese.

I was so full at the end of the smorgasbord of ice cream tastes, but I fell hard for Midnight Madness. I ordered up a small scoop and walked out feeling quite satisfied and happy with this First.

The ice cream parlor First is a metaphor for this entire journey of new things. You've got to take little tastes of everything. And what's true for ice cream tasting is true for life; you just never know what you're going to like.

Enjoy the tasting marathon.

Other Firsts Like This to Try

◊ Try every flavor at a yogurt store where you can serve up your own. Again, use caution. Small samples.

◇ Take a bite of *every* food at an all-you-can-eat buffet.

◇ Order all the appetizers on the menu.

Drive with No Planned Destination: Day 238

You have to leave the city of your comfort and go into the wilderness of your intuition. What you'll discover will be wonderful. What you'll discover is yourself.

—ALAN ALDA

I know people who just like to drive. I know other people who like to drive aimlessly when they can't deal with whatever is going on in their house and they need to escape. I am neither of these kinds of people.

I am the person who always likes to know exactly where I'm going at all times. I usually arm myself with a GPS, maps, and Google Maps printout directions before I drive anywhere I haven't been before. I like to have backup plans for my backup plans, and I hate being lost at any time.

This may be the result of years of TV news reporting. Getting lost means you lose time, miss your deadline, or don't get the story. Also, driving into the wrong neighborhood can lead you to a scene right out of *The Bonfires of the Vanities*. I once ended up at a motorcycle gang's clubhouse and had a gun pointed at my head. I tried to explain I took a wrong turn. That didn't go over well. I stepped on the gas and ended up lost and crying, and I didn't get the story either. I'm just telling you this so you know I'm not completely crazy, I've just had a few weird things happen that make me want to know EXACTLY where I'm going.

So, while this First is as easy as stepping on the gas, I did have to fight everything in me to leave all maps behind, just let go, and drive with absolutely no destination in mind. (Okay, I did bring my cell phone with a GPS just to make sure I could get home.)

I filled the tank with gas, turned up the radio, and headed west of Philadelphia, driving familiar roads for only about ten minutes until I turned onto one I'd never been on before.

It was a good turn. The road took me into a beautiful, lush-looking forest area. You couldn't see many houses for all the trees. It felt far from the city, and it wasn't long before I saw a sign for Tyler Arboretum. I'd never been there before. I wasn't really sure where I was. I decided to just follow the signs.

It was a beautiful warm day, perfect for a walk in the Arboretum. I found myself on a trail dotted with gnomes and little fairy houses built by local artists. I moved farther down the path, ending up in a grove of unique tree houses. This was much more of an adventure than I'd expected. I was tagging along behind a group of little kids scrambling through the treetop homes, all different, modern, rustic, traditional, or quirky. They each provided a spectacular view of the arboretum. The kids were giggling as they discovered every fun twist and turn in the arbor architecture, and I found myself smiling too.

The trail eventually led to a screened-in butterfly house. I entered through a gate, holding out my hand to see if one would land on me. It occurred to me that we always associate butterflies with freedom, but here they were being held captive in a lovely but enclosed garden. I, however, was free of maps, plans, exact coordinates, flying with no instruments or boundaries.

I'd imagined that my journey had taken me far from home. In fact, when I got back in my car and checked the GPS, I was stunned to find I was less than 10 miles from where I'd started. I'd just taken a different turn.

You know I was channeling poet Robert Frost, right? Two roads? "I took the one less traveled by." It does make all the difference.

We often travel the same paths in our lives, literally and figuratively. Firsts are about getting off that well-worn path. Strike off on a different trail for a new, fresh view. As this little adventure proved to me, you don't have to wander far to find new roads in your life worth exploring.

Other Firsts Like This to Try

◊ Walk somewhere instead of driving. Walk to work. Same streets; different view.

◊ Always take the highway? Take the scenic route.

◊ Take your gym workout outside. Find a park you've never been to before. Roam or run the trails solo or with a friend.

Final Thoughts

Easy Firsts let you juggle work, family, school, and activities while forcing you to light the fire of your imagination, creativity, and uniqueness. They add texture and depth to everyday life and give you the confidence to try big challenging Firsts. Finding all the opportunities for new experiences around you just whets your appetite for more. Once you open the window of your life through small, easy Firsts, it will feel like breathing in fresh air. This is a chance to test, try, sample, make trial runs for no other reason than that you can. And in doing that you will begin to imagine all the other things you'd like to try—all the other possibilities.

TIPS FOR FINDING YOUR EASY FIRSTS

- Change up your routine. Routine is comforting, but it also buries us in layers of sameness. Always walk around the block the same way? Stop. Go a different way. Push yourself to be a little less predictable. Today you will *not* have "the usual."

- Sometimes when we feel stuck, we feel isolated. Introduce yourself to someone you see all the time at home or work but don't know their name. You'll be surprised how good it feels to extend yourself a little. Don't be embarrassed. They've probably been thinking about introducing themselves to you. Be the First.

- Take just five to fifteen minutes to organize something for the first time. You might need to invest in a drawer divider or a new basket or container. Once it's done, you might be surprised by how much time it saves you from hunting for something. You'll feel less stressed. It's something you can control. It makes life easier.

CHAPTER 3

Just Say "Yes"

Invitation Firsts

Before I started my Year of Firsts I'd gotten into the habit of saying "No."

My husband . . . "Want to try a new restaurant in the city?"

"No. I don't want to deal with parking. Let's stay home."

Coworker . . . "I'm going to a new art festival. Come with me."

"No thanks. I have plans."

I knew, intuitively, "No" was part of the reason I was stuck. The word "No" had to go. I was tripping over it. To do daily Firsts I realized I had to do a real-life version of Jim Carrey's movie *Yes Man* and just say "Yes" to as many invitations as possible, even if I didn't think I wanted to do it.

So I did. I said "Yes" to an Irish hooley, though I had no idea what that was at the time. I said "Yes" to teaching a college course, though I had no idea how I would fit it in my schedule.

I said "Yes" to being a clown, even though I have a clown phobia, "Yes" to learning to row on the river, "Yes" to getting dunked in a dunk tank.

While I was learning to say that three-letter word, trust me, lots of four-letter words came out of my mouth too. It just wasn't easy to say "Yes" when my initial thought automatically went to my default "No."

But I started to find the more often I said "Yes," the more it felt like the pieces of a puzzle started to fit together. I was creating a new life out of "Yes."

My *10! Show* guest booker Jami Osiecki cheered me on as I tackled one new First after another. She was often the instigator of ideas:

"Hey the drummer from the Hooters is coming on the show. Want to take a drum lesson?"

"Yes."

"Want to go to a Chinese fortune cookie factory?"

"Yes."

"Want to learn how to make sushi?"

"Yes."

While I said "Yes" to everything she could dream up, Jami was stuck in "No."

Jami is a sweet, smart, dark-haired beauty with doe eyes and an angel face. Plenty of male celebrities who came on the show were immediately smitten with her. But Jami was generally unimpressed and admittedly unhappy.

Jami talked about wanting to be married. She wanted to have children, but prior bad relationships haunted her. She was at a point in her life where she said "No" a lot.

One day she told me about this guy who kept asking her to

go out for a drink. He was a former high school classmate. She would say "Yes" and then make some excuse and reschedule. One day, she told me she was about to cancel on him a third time.

"Why?"

"I just don't feel like it. If I hate him, then I'm stuck and I won't be able to leave. I'm tired. I just want to go home."

"What are you going to do at home?"

"I don't know, but I just won't have to deal with another disappointment, which this is sure to be. What's the point?"

I recognized and sympathized with Jami's thinking. I understood how "No" was predictable and safe. But I'd reached a turning point, ironically with Jami's help, appreciating all the possibilities that came with the word "Yes."

"Just say 'Yes,' Jami. Just say 'Yes,' and if you don't like this guy, you've lost absolutely nothing. Give yourself permission to leave in a half hour. Who knows? You might like him. He might be the one. But I can assure you, if you go home, absolutely nothing new will happen and you will be as bored and disappointed as you are this minute."

Jami stopped and looked at me. I know that she'd been trying so hard to protect herself from any more pain, but in the process she knew she'd stopped taking chances.

"Okay. Okay. For you, Lu Ann, I'm going to say 'Yes.' I'll go."

I thought, *No, for you, Jami, you're saying "Yes."* I crossed my fingers, just hoping she'd have a nice time. Nothing more.

The next morning I asked, "How'd it go?"

She was smiling. "Good!"

"Really!?"

"I liked him."

"Ha-ha . . ." I danced around the office. "Jami liked him!"

"I did. I might see him again." She was laughing now too.

Her smile was infectious. Everyone on the staff grooved and basked in her morning glow. And it never stopped. Just like something out of a mushy chick flick movie, Jami Osiecki, the girl who said she was always in the wrong relationship, found herself in the right one. Weeks and months passed and Jami was still smiling. I'd never seen her like this. We all felt happy because she deserved something wonderful in her life.

I knew it was getting serious when Jami told me she was going on vacation with her "boyfriend Neil" and they were going to fly to Vegas. She dreads flying, but Jami told me Neil promised he would hold her hand and the barf bag if necessary and she agreed to do it. If that isn't true love, I don't know what is. Another big First!

No, they did not get married in Vegas, but it wasn't long after that Neil bent down on one knee at a concert in New York City. He arranged for Jami to be serenaded in public with the song "One in a Million You" when he proposed.

One year after she first said "Yes" to meeting Neil, I witnessed Jami say "I do."

Jami is still grinning ear to ear today and just told me "We're pregnant!" I like to believe she and Neil would have found each other eventually no matter what. Surely, it must have been fate. Still, I think "Yes" gave fate a little nudge.

Not every "Yes" will rock and change your world like this, but you never know. Think about how many times you say "No" during a day; how many times friends, family, or coworkers invite you to do something and you reject it. If you're stuck and you are trying to figure out how to start making changes in

HERE'S SOME SCIENTIFIC EVIDENCE
THAT SAYING "YES" WILL IMPROVE YOUR LIFE

- Say "Yes" to new social situations. Numerous studies show that extroverts and introverts experience more happiness when they are in social gatherings. If you are an introvert, you may need to push yourself a little harder knowing, like eating your vegetables, it's good for you.

- Say "Yes" to getting to know someone new. A University of Michigan study shows a friendly conversation will improve your cognitive abilities and make it easier to solve common problems.

- A study of rats (yes, another rodent study) by a Princeton researcher suggests positive social interaction can buffer the physiological effects of stress.

your life immediately, dare yourself to say "Yes" to your next invitation. I assure you, something different will happen.

Be a Clown: Day 33

If you change the way you look at things, the things you look at change.
—WAYNE DYER

First, I want to preface this clown adventure with an apology to all professional and amateur clowns. I'm sorry, but I've always been a little clown phobic. I'm not sure why, but as a kid I freaked out and cried anytime I saw a painted face and big red nose. Water-squirting flowers and balloon animals only made things worse.

I carried my "clown issues" into adulthood. When my daughter was born, a friend gave us a beautiful, circus-colored two-foot-long paper-mache full-bodied clown for her room. I put him on a shelf near my daughter's crib, but was soon convinced he was casting some evil shadow. It wasn't long before I had to just stuff him in a closet. I think he eventually left by way of a garage sale.

I had to tell you that back story so you understand why I hesitated when ShoBo Da Clown invited me to a clown meeting. "Be a clown," he said. "We'll teach you balloon tricks." I didn't have the heart to tell him the idea made me slightly queasy.

Still, what could I do? I had to face my clown fear and accept his sincere invitation.

When I walked into the meeting in a South Jersey church, I was relieved to see a room full of very nice, normal-looking people—no one "clowning around" (forgive me). But everyone was all abuzz because tonight's monthly gathering was dedicated to learning to put on perfect clown makeup. They asked if I would like to be a model.

Inside, I was thinking *RUN!*

Instead, I said, "Sure! Absolutely!"

I felt a bit ashamed as I heard one of the women tell the group about how important it is to make children laugh and how "some" parents make their kids anxious by saying "Now, don't be afraid of the clown."

Oh no. Is that why I was afraid? Did I pass my fear on to my daughter?

Some of the more experienced clowns demonstrated how to transform into a funny sweet girl clown, or a hobo clown, or a traditional Bozo-type clown. I saw what an art it is to get "into character."

Ha, I thought, *clown phobia therapy.*

And then it was my turn. The clown artists worked their magic on me. In less than a half hour, it was *show time* for Lu Lu the clown.

I laughed out loud when I looked in the mirror. Was that me? A bright red curly wig with a tiny hat surrounded my white face, with a little red heart on my nose and cupid lips. Awww. I think Lu Lu the clown was kind of adorable. Not scary at all. Everyone took pictures and I embraced my inner clown among ShoBo and new friends. I even learned how to make a balloon dog.

At the end of the meeting, I took off my clown wig, gave everyone a hug, and headed home. When I came to the toll bridge to cross over to Philly, I had completely forgotten I was still essentially Lu Lu the clown, wearing a full face of makeup.

You should have seen the toll taker's expression. I'm not sure if he was startled, amused, or both. He eventually smiled. My "Yes" to a clown face made someone else smile. I smiled too, all the way home.

Other Firsts Like This to Try

◊ Say "Yes" to a costume party.

◊ Say "Yes" to being in a fund-raiser fashion show.

◊ Say "Yes" to playing Santa or an elf.

Dance at an Irish Hooley: Day 65

The only way to make sense out of change is to plunge into it, move with it, and join the dance.
—ALAN WATTS

"What the heck is an Irish hooley?" I asked my husband, Phil, who has plenty of Irish in him.

"No idea," he said.

"Well, I've accepted an invitation to go to one."

"Oi, good luck to you, lassie," he said in his best fake Irish brogue, "you'll be on your own. I'm playing racquetball tonight."

Nothing like going to a dance without a dance partner, but John and Jaqueline Kelly of the South Jersey Irish Society assured me that wasn't a problem at an Irish hooley.

I heard a loud Irish jig as I walked into the Palmyra Knights of Columbus Hall, and before I could take my coat off I was grabbed by both hands and swung into something akin to a square dance.

"Whoa! I don't know how to do this," I tried yelling over the music to the older gentleman who now linked his arm in mine and was twirling me around.

He just motioned me to start clapping and change partners. The room was packed with about a hundred people. A live Irish band was playing, and I was thrust into a group of eight dancing, smiling adults and children.

Within minutes I was laughing, hair flying, going the wrong

way, being pushed the right way, having no idea where I was supposed to go next. No one cared. Someone threw a green boa on me, and after a few times around, I started to channel my sixth-grade square dancing class. Or was it like the Israeli dancing I had tried? No, it was a combo of both, like peanut butter and chocolate.

I thought, *Okay, this move is like do-si-do your partner. And this move is like the horah!*

Whatever it was, it was joyous and passionate. No wallflowers allowed. No formal introductions necessary. You're at a hooley? You dance!

Eventually, I took a breather to get some water. John and Jaqueline came by to check on me to make sure I was having a good time.

"Are you kidding? How can you not have a good time? Thank you so much for inviting me."

And I was off again. Now, I let all caution go, holding hands with whoever stood on either side, skipping and circling, charging into the middle, swinging from one arm to the next, heart pounding, laughing at my missteps.

I kept thinking of the Jewish toast "L'chaim . . . to life."

That's what I felt, anyway, at my First Irish hooley: The Irish get it. Life must be celebrated with carefree music and dancing. We forget that sometimes. We forget how to join in the circle.

Ha. L'chaim, I thought when I left. *That's what a hooley is.*

⬦ Say "Yes" to every single dance at a wedding party. Invite someone else to dance.

⬦ Say "Yes" to doing a public happy dance. Invite others to join.

⬦ Say "Yes" to a ballroom dance class.

Parade and Sing with Barbershop Quartet: Day 183

If you wait for inspiration, you'll be standing on the corner after the parade is a mile down the street.

—BEN NICHOLAS

I call Noel Dickson my "cousin." The truth is he *was* married to my cousin, then got divorced, but *I* refuse to "divorce" him because he's always so much fun.

He lives in Cincinnati, so I rarely see him except at some oddball big family gathering where he's still invited.

Noel's been a performing artist and teacher for as long as I've known him. But I was completely taken aback when I found out his latest passion is barbershop chorus singing.

Hmmm . . . quirky, I thought. (No offense intended, Barbershop enthusiasts.) Noel called me to say he was coming to Philadelphia for a big Barbershop Convention.

"Come see me perform," he invited.

"Only if you can help me with a First," I told him. I knew Noel would come up with something good.

When I showed up at the convention hall, Noel was rehearsing with the Southern Gateway Chorus. Strangely, not a sound was coming out of their mouths. Have you ever seen a hundred grown men pantomime the song "Ma, She's Making Eyes at Me"? Weird. Apparently, they were saving their vocal chords for the competition.

As per our agreement, Noel arranged a First for me. After rehearsal, he taught me how to sing a song ending called a "tag" and he worked me into a little number with his barbershop friends. Ha! I loved it! I was completely off tune but actually found myself truly enjoying the challenge of the team harmony. Once again, Noel proved why he's my favorite, not real cousin, cousin.

But, the best invitation came the next day. Noel called to say his chorus was asked to perform "God Bless America" in the big Independence Day Parade in Philly. Whoo Hoo! He was allowed to bring a guest (moi!) to sing and march alongside him. I just had to wear something red, white, and blue and wave a flag.

I've lost count of the years I have covered this parade as a news reporter from the sidelines. I never imagined being a part of it.

My husband brought his camera. The video still makes me smile. We were so into it, parading down the streets of Philadelphia. We sang "God Bless America" fifteen times. Each time I was singing louder, competing with Noel, kind of in harmony, as people clapped and cheered us on. I loved every minute of it.

I have to say, I owe Cousin Noel big-time for the experience.

"Yes" once again took me somewhere I never expected to go. I was no longer an observer. I was a participant.

How often do we watch life go by and think we're living? It's so much more fun to be in the parade, passionately doing something. Why be a bystander? Sing at the top of your lungs. Say "Yes" and jump into the parade of life.

Other Firsts Like This to Try

⬦ Say "Yes" to see friends or family perform: sing, dance, play an instrument.

⬦ Say "Yes" to any friend who will share their hobby with you: fish, knit, sew, golf.

⬦ Say "Yes" to being in or helping to organize a neighborhood parade.

Dunked by Young Readers: Day 227

A small group of thoughtful people could change the world. Indeed, it's the only thing that ever has.
—MARGARET MEAD

A lot of people think being a TV news reporter or anchor is a glamorous job. Sometimes it is. However, I can assure you that when my alarm went off at 3:30 a.m. on this particular Saturday morning, I didn't feel glamorous. I felt cursed. I also felt nauseous.

I couldn't remember why I agreed to fill in and solo anchor four hours of early morning news. Even if you work the shift full-time (which I've done), your body never gets used to it.

As I was trying to pry my eyes open while applying fake lashes, I remembered this was also the day I'd agreed to get dunked in a dunk tank. Now, I wanted to cry.

What was I thinking when I agreed to all of this? Oh, I know. I said I would accept invitations to do something for the first time. Great.

I wish I could tell you that every day of my yearlong journey was inspirational and I never thought about quitting, but I'd be lying. There were days when I wanted to crawl back into bed and tell my friends *Yeah, that was a crazy idea, huh? But now I'm done with it.*

This was one of those days.

It was noon when I started driving to the Indian Valley Public Library in Telford, Pennsylvania. I'd gotten out of my "anchor clothes" and changed into a bathing suit and shorts. The whole drive I was talking to myself: *You can do this. A dunk in a tank might be refreshing. You made a promise. You are going to keep it. Just keep going.*

You know, sometimes you just get lucky in spite of yourself. I was lucky this day. I was cranky and tired on my way to the library, but everything changed the moment I got there.

I was greeted by Lindy Janson and Sarah Figueroa. I don't know how to explain how lovely, sweet, and dedicated these librarians are to the children they serve. They would do anything to get kids to read, even get dunked in a dunk tank.

And so on this day, dozens of children who read more than ten books over the summer were told they could dunk their favorite librarian plus me. Truly, these little ones had no idea who I was or why I was invited to the dunking party. The kids graciously agreed to dunk me (the stranger) anyway.

I'd been dragging and whining. Now I was laughing, nervous, sitting on the end of a miniature diving board contraption hanging over a four-foot-deep dunk tank.

Oh Yea. Bring it on! I thought as I waited for my first young reader to take a shot at dunking me.

But before anyone could toss the first bean bag at the big dunk button . . . *Plop! Splash! AHHHHHH!* I was in the water.

What happened? I screamed and laughed.

Apparently I'd squirmed too much on the board and it collapsed on its own, surprising the heck out of everyone.

Okay, well, now I know what I'm in for.

I tentatively climbed back up and sat on the board, anticipating my next dunking. The dunk machine had a mind of its own, though. Sometimes it failed to dunk me when it was supposed to. Sometimes, it just unexpectedly dropped me in the water. The kids loved the unpredictable dunkings and the look on my face. We were all laughing.

When I left, the librarians were still being dunked, and I didn't feel tired anymore. I felt inspired and happy and glad there are people like Lindsay and Sarah in the world, glad to know they've helped create a safe, nurturing haven for the children in their community.

I know I was slaphappy and delirious by the time I got home. But I had to admit, a good dunking in ice water was exactly what I needed.

◊ Say "Yes" to jumping in the pool with all your clothes on.

◊ Say "Yes" to a pillow fight.

◊ Say "Yes" to a Super Soaker water gun party.

Row on the River: Day 234

Merrily, merrily, merrily, merrily, life is but a dream. . . .
— "ROW, ROW, ROW YOUR BOAT"

A river runs through Philadelphia. It is rarely more beautiful than when the sun is just barely peeking up on the city skyline and you can watch dozens of rowing teams in their boats, gliding on the Schuylkill. From Martin Luther King Drive running parallel to the river, you can sometimes hear the oars dipping into the water in unison, a voice through a bullhorn, a coxswain counting strokes.

Though the whole city can see it, I would guess most believe as I did: You have to be part of "the club" to be welcomed into this iconic Philadelphia sport. I always assumed rowing was an activity reserved for Philadelphia's wealthy and privileged. Not me. What's a girl who grew up in Atlanta know about rowing? Nothing! I never rowed. But I was envious. It looked so graceful, so magical; four or eight people in a sleek boat moving in unison, skimming the water. I wondered what it was like.

So it happened during my Year of Firsts, I received a rowing invitation that piqued my interest. An enthusiastic rower, Judy Hasday, followed my blog and emailed, *Come to Philadelphia's Access to Rowing and Paddling Day!* Her organization was trying to get people like me to try it.

Okay. Finally! I get to see what this rowing thing is all about.

I told Judy to sign me up. The experience included a free lesson on land and then real rowing time on the river with other first-timers and an instructor.

I couldn't have planned a more gorgeous day to be on the river. The sun was shining. The temperature was just a little cool. I started in a boathouse on an indoor rower, learning the motion, leaning forward, sweeping the oars through the imaginary water, pulling back and forward. There's supposed to be a natural rhythm to this, but nothing about it felt natural to me. My oars flailed around like flapping arms. Who knew rowing a boat was so complicated?

I met two other women around my age who were lovely and just as clueless about this. Mary Catherine Dabrowski said she was on a dragon boat team (very different) and always wanted to try this. Naisha Walton was from out of town and was trying to experience "everything Philly." When presented with a skinny two-foot-wide boat at the dock, we unanimously worried out loud that there was no way our butts could possibly fit on the teeny tiny little bony skeletal-looking seats.

We were wrong (that made us all feel much better about our rear ends). But getting seated in the boat was still a major balancing challenge. It felt like trying to sit down on a rolling log. We all laughed, knowing this virgin row could be disastrous, but what the heck. We were in the boat. Local college student Chris Miller was our fourth. His job was to keep us in the boat. As Scooby Doo would say, "Rets row!"

One by one, we were coached from a motorized launch boat shadowing us. A voice we heard through a megaphone shouted: "Rowing is a feeling. Close your eyes, Lu Ann. Now, get the feeling." Generally, anytime someone tells me to close my eyes, I just get nervous. Yet, I did start to "feel" it.

I opened my eyes again as we eased by ducks and geese and water plants. I couldn't help but think the city looked and felt different from the river. Nature seemed closer. It was almost peaceful, even though you could hear the hum of traffic nearby. There was something soothing in the rhythmic row.

My novice teammates and I all felt it—we were a little transformed and awed by the experience. But after a good hour on the water, we were also tired. A brain and a body can only take in so much brand-new information at a time. When we got to the dock, we were ready for solid ground.

"Would you do it again?" I asked Naisha and Mary Catherine. They agreed they would, but we also had an appreciation for the training, discipline, and time it would take to actually be good at this. None of us were ready to make the commitment.

Still, I felt buoyed and at ease as I left the boathouse. It was a good workout. I met interesting people. I saw my city from a whole new perspective. I gave Judy a hug and a thank-you for the invite.

I could be a part of this . . . I thought. And now I know, because *I felt the row.*

◊ Say "Yes" to renting any kind of boat for the day: paddleboat, rowboat, speedboat.

◊ Say "Yes" to an indoor rowing exercise class.

◊ Say "Yes" to trying horseback riding, yoga, polo, rugby, racquetball, squash.

Final Thoughts

It may be difficult to start saying "Yes" when you've spent years saying "No." "No" may have been an answer that worked for you in the past, but if you are stuck and every day seems the same, saying "Yes" will help change that. "Yes" means you will take more risks. "Yes" means you will accept invitations to do things that take you outside your comfort zone. "Yes" takes you into social situations you may not be sure of. But "Yes" will also take you down a new path of what could be, what might happen. As I told my friend Jami, we know where "No" leads us. We have no idea where "Yes" can take us. It could be somewhere wonderful.

TIPS FOR FINDING INVITATION FIRSTS

- Let everyone in your life know you will say "Yes" to all invitations (unless it's dangerous or conflicts with your personal code of ethics).

- If you are invited at work or there is an opportunity to try a new assignment or learn a new skill, jump in; say "Yes."

- If someone you know is organizing a trip, a class for something you've never tried, say "Yes."

- You don't have to wait for a personal invitation. There are websites online that organize social activities that are open to anyone. You just have to sign up. Some activities are free. Some might require an activity fee.

- Start with one day. Take note of how many times you say "No" to invitations large and small during the day. Pick a day to say "Yes" to everything.

- It might feel like you aren't sure why you are agreeing to do things you don't even know if you're interested in. That's okay. Just do it anyway. Then, don't be surprised when something comes along that you've always hoped for, something that you've always wanted to say "Yes" to.

CHAPTER 4

Go Somewhere! Do Something!

Firsts That Move You

As the months went by during my Year of Firsts, I felt more joy; I felt more present every day. I knew I was moving in a positive direction. But of course, life happens—events I couldn't control, painful days that made me cry. Some of those days, out of necessity, became my Firsts. I didn't always want to blog about them. It felt like pulling off a layer of skin. Still, I knew I had to take the good and the bad as part of my journey.

On Day 146, I said good-bye to my work partner of eighteen years, TV news photographer Dave Bentley. That's the day he called it quits at the station. We shared years of stakeouts, awards, friendship. I watched him get married and have babies. He was there when I had surgeries and was fighting cancer. We always had each other's back.

If I was doing a First during work, Dave was often dragged into being my droll sidekick. He was much better than me at reciting the alphabet backwards, and he embarrassed me when I tried to pay the bridge toll of the people driving behind us.

But things at work had changed so drastically with cutbacks and resources, he said he just couldn't hang in anymore. I completely understood. His wife, my friend Connie, wanted to move to Phoenix with their two kids. Dave was among a dozen smart, experienced, veteran journalists who left our newsroom that year, some taking buyouts. I couldn't blame them, but I felt sad and in some ways abandoned.

Just over a month later, we put our dog Angel to sleep. Angel was a golden retriever—border collie mix, and I can tell you she was no angel. She was one mess of a dog. She hated other dogs. My husband Phil and I could barely walk around the block without her almost ripping the leash out of our hands to go attack some innocent pooch across the street. But she adored babies. She loved people. And while my daughter may have been the one who picked her from a mistake litter that a breeder didn't want, Angel was really always my dog.

Like everyone else in my life, Angel was often coerced into taking part in a First. She was in my video on the day I made snow angels. One day I brushed her dog teeth with some peanut butter toothpaste. She put up with me trying to teach her how to high-five. I didn't realize these were some of her last days. Maybe I didn't want to.

She was twelve, so she had slowed down, but I was stunned when I was told she had a cancerous tumor that was inoperable. In the end, she cried in pain. My husband and I cried with her on the floor at the vet's office until they gave her heavy painkillers. We didn't want to let her go. I watched her eyes close for the last time and felt the deepest grief.

Angel was gone, but I still kept expecting to see her greet me at the door. For a second, I'd forget. Home didn't feel right without her. Meanwhile, the workplace that had always seemed like my second home felt strange to me too. I felt at a loss some days.

Oddly, while the floor felt like it was shifting beneath me, my daily new First experiences were the constant in my life that kept me going. Some days, I'm sure they were a distraction from what I didn't want to think about and what I couldn't control.

After Angel died, we went back to our annual family reunion in St. Augustine, Florida. Firsts were easy there. I just had to play tourist. I climbed the lighthouse I'd always looked at from a distance. I went to the alligator farm I'd never visited. I fished for the first time with our nieces and nephews off the pier. I flew a two-handed kite.

I just kept moving—taking long walks along the ocean, allowing time to mourn what felt like losses. But also breathing deep, taking in the ocean air, reminding myself all things change. I would have to change. I needed to evolve and go forward.

Returning home, I felt refreshed and tried to get my bearings again. Earlier in the year, my friend Loraine Ballard-Morrill introduced me to a group of women who call themselves the "Damsels in Success." I laughed out loud when she asked me to join. I called it her "Damsels in 'Distress'" group. I insisted I wasn't joining a club with such a ridiculous name. But Loraine was persistent.

"Come on," she said. "It will be a First, and I promise you'll like these women."

Reluctantly I agreed. After all, I'd promised myself to say "Yes."

I met the Damsels at a French crepe restaurant in Philly I'd never been to before. So far so good. Kelly Green, the DIS founder, is a fireball of energy and a charity fund-raiser. Members introduced themselves: a nonprofit attorney, an aide to the mayor, a school board member. Despite the silly name, these were all substantial women with interesting lives. I didn't think the whole thing was so silly anymore.

At first, I didn't attend many "Damsel" meetings." But when I felt at a loss to understand all the changes happening around me, I realized I was comforted by the lives and experiences of this group of women. I wasn't alone.

By the middle of the year, I was a regular. There are about thirty Damsels, but the beauty of the group is that you never know who is going to show up. Every meeting is a different combination. I'm still meeting some of the members and we often move the meeting to different restaurants for first-time experiences.

The group supported my mission of Firsts, giving me ideas and sometimes getting into the act. Phoebe met me for a Segway tour around the art museum. Kelly made me a ticket seller at a charity event. Loraine joined me for a contemporary dance class.

In the past, I might have shut down and closed out family and friends when I was feeling down. Moving Firsts forced me to do the opposite, and having new friends and experiences to draw from kept me going.

Admittedly, it takes more mental effort to get up off your

STUDIES SUGGESTING GOING SOMEWHERE NEW IS GOOD FOR YOU

- David Eagleman, a professor of neuroscience at Houston's Baylor College of Medicine, did a study showing when you go somewhere you've been before the memories are "compressed"; time flies. But everything slows down when traveling to a new place. The brain experiences things more fully, kind of like a sponge, like a child experiencing something brand-new.

- Professor Adam Gallinsky at the Kellogg School of Management at Northwest University says his study shows people who travel or go somewhere new will often have "epiphanies" because they put some psychological distance between themselves and their normal environment. You don't have to go far. Any new place allows you to step away from your daily living and gives you a different perspective or insight you might not have gained otherwise.

behind and go out when you're in a funk. That is exactly why you should go. Just going somewhere new, walking into some different environment lifts you. All you have to do is get there, take it in, and experience it. Let Firsts be your inspiration to go, to move your life in a better direction.

Walk Across the Ben Franklin Bridge: Day 27

Walking is good for solving problems—it's like the feet are little psychiatrists.
—PEPPER GIARDINO

The Ben Franklin Bridge is a mile and a half span crossing the Delaware River between Philadelphia and Camden, New Jersey. It's old and painted blue, but sometimes when the sunset is full of pink and orange, the combination of bridge, water, and sparkling lights of Philly's Center City make it all seem like an enchanting picturesque gateway.

I have seen this view a thousand times, crossing the river in a news truck, heading home after finishing a story in Jersey. I know that lovely image is a kind of a mirage, because the truth is, in the hard light of day, the bridge is a gritty traffic-jammed connector, physically touching down in two hardscrabble worlds.

When someone suggested I walk the bridge for a First, I was surprised. All these years in Philadelphia and I didn't know you could walk the bridge. I didn't recall seeing anyone do it. I was assured it was true: Along the six lanes of bridge traffic was a pedestrian walkway.

Don't ask me why I decided to try this in January. It was one of those days I wasn't sure what I would do for a First. I was shooting part of a story in Jersey and waiting to interview someone in Philly. I had an hour or so to kill. My sidekick photographer Dave Bentley wanted lunch.

"Tell you what. Drop me off at the foot of the bridge. You go grab some lunch. I'll meet you on the other side in Philly," I said.

"What, are you nuts? It's freezing. It's going to be even colder on the bridge."

"I don't care. I need a First today. This is it. Come with me if you want."

"That's ridiculous. Then we'd both be walking back and forth across the bridge to get back to the car. No, thanks. You really are nuts. Call me when you get to the other side you looney tune."

I was still in the first month of Firsts, and Dave was not sure why I was doing this and why I had to involve him at any point. He did know me well enough to know that I was stubborn as hell and would not be talked out of this bridge walk. He dropped me off and headed over the bridge.

The sky was blue, but the wind was blowing. Dave was right of course. It was much colder up on the bridge. I was wearing a winter coat over a dress and I was in heels. Not really appropriate clothes for the walk. Nevertheless, I was determined.

The cold wind and the view looking over the river took my breath away at first. You can't see this perspective from your car. It's a long way down to the water. I ran into two joggers running the bridge for exercise. They were dressed from head to toe in spandex winter running gear.

"You do this all the time? How long does it take?" My ears were getting cold and my heels were slipping into the walkway cracks.

"Well, we go pretty fast. It takes us about ten minutes each way."

In heels I figured this would take me about triple that time. I kept walking.

I was about halfway over when I heard something coming up behind me. I turned around to see a police officer on a bike. His name was Michael Jackson. No joke.

"Hi," he said. "Why are you walking the bridge?"

"Why?"

"Yeah. You don't really look dressed for this."

"Uh, well, this might sound a little crazy, but I'm doing this for a first-time experience."

"Are you crazy?"

"Maybe. Can I take some video of you for my blog?"

"I guess so."

Officer Jackson stayed with me, and then I realized he really thought something might be wrong with me.

"Do you ride alongside everyone who comes across the bridge?"

"No. You just didn't seem like someone taking a jog up here."

The light went on. "Did you think I was a jumper?"

"Well, I've seen a few go down." He wasn't laughing. He was serious.

"Oh no, no, no. I'm not jumping."

"When someone comes walking up in heels," he explained, "you just don't know."

I hadn't thought of that. In the TV news business, we generally don't report suicides. Apparently part of Officer Jackson's job was trying to prevent them. I asked how many he'd seen, but now he'd realized I was a reporter. He was very nice but he didn't want to say.

He followed me to the end of the bridge. He still seemed concerned.

"How are you leaving here?"

"Oh, my photographer is picking me up."

Officer Jackson shook my hand and seemed relieved.

I now was imagining someone on the bridge, maybe on one of those pretty sunset nights thinking this was a fine way to go out. The thought gave me chills.

Dave picked me up and asked how my walk was.

"Oh great. I met an officer who thought I was going to jump."

Dave laughed. "Oh boy. I told you it was a crazy idea. Who goes up on that bridge dressed like you are?"

I laughed too. I thought of the irony, someone believing I might want to end my life when in fact I couldn't have felt more invigorated by the panoramic view from on high of two cities, the blue sky, the cold wind slapping me in the face, making my nose run and my ears burn.

I couldn't have felt more alive.

Other Firsts Like This to Try

◊ Go to the top of the tallest building in your town.

◊ Visit on foot a landmark you've driven by many times for a different view.

◊ Go to an amusement park you've never been to before.

Go to the Opera: Day 133

There's no half-singing in the shower, you're either a rock star or an opera diva.
—JOSH GROBAN

There are definitely gaps in my cultural experience. Opera was one of them. I actually felt kind of guilty about it, considering I live in a city that birthed the first opera house in America. I knew eventually I had to right this cultural wrong. But for some reason I wasn't really motivated until my friend and coworker Kristen Welker suggested it as a First. She had an "in" with some tickets.

"Figaro, Figaro, Figaro . . . ?" That's all that popped into my head.

Kristen says, "Nope. It's Verdi's *La Traviata*."

"Oh." No clue.

"It means fallen woman. It's the story of a courtesan who falls in love with a gentleman and dies in the end with lots of Shakespearean kind of twists in the middle."

"Oh. Fallen woman? Exciting. Scandalous. But it's in Italian, right? Will I understand anything going on?"

"Sure. The Philadelphia Academy of Music puts up English subtitles throughout the performance."

"Super."

My husband, Phil, came with me to the opera. We were fascinated with the crowd that gathered for this performance: an elegant group speaking with hushed anticipation about the performance. Definitely Philadelphia society that I didn't often rub shoulders with.

I was being introduced around.

"Hello, my dear, so nice to meet you. How is it possible you've never been to the opera?"

I laughed nervously. "No idea. But I'm really looking forward to it." *Am I?*

"You are going to love it. This opera has so much drama. The costuming is superb."

The Academy of Music is a gorgeous theater with red velvet-covered seats and gilded wood sculptures everywhere, and just as grand as you would imagine the first opera house in America would be. We had wonderful seats in the balcony, looking onto center stage. The lights went down. The orchestra started playing. The curtain went up.

This is where my memory gets kind of hazy. I do know by the time the "fallen woman" died in her lover's arms, I was confused. *Didn't she die already?* The costumes and sets were opulent. The singing voices were fabulously operatic. But mostly I remember my eyes drooping and trying to keep up and follow the subtitles projected above the "action" on the stage.

I want to like this, I thought. *I want to say, I love the opera. Why can't I make my brain enjoy this?*

During the intermission, I woke up. *What did everyone think?* I heard someone stand up shouting "Bravo." I heard someone else say the production was "uninspiring." I had no idea which it was. Phil had no idea either.

I looked at him and quietly whispered, "Are we just uncultured bumpkins?"

"Don't know. Maybe you have to be brought up on it."

We graciously thanked Kristen and our host who gave us tickets. I think I might have said it was a "once in a lifetime experience," which it probably was.

And that's okay. That's what part of the First experience is really about. Finding out what doesn't thrill you is important too. Opera didn't move me. Go figure. It might move you to tears. You never know, until you go. At the very least, I'm proud to say I'm not an opera virgin anymore.

Other Firsts Like This to Try

◊ Go to a free concert in the park.

◊ Go to a free museum day. Check online for dates.

◊ Make a list of your cultural gaps. Ballet? Classical concert? Just go.

Yoga for Living Beyond Breast Cancer: Day 137

You gain strength, courage and confidence by every experience in which you really stop to look fear in the face.
—ELEANOR ROOSEVELT

Sometimes a "go" First is a place you go in your mind and heart. For this First, I thought I was going to a breast cancer survivor event I'd never been to before. It turned out to be much more than that.

As of this writing, I'm a twenty-one-year survivor. I tell women who have just been diagnosed with breast cancer, the first year is war. You go to battle for your life. There's surgery, chemo, hair loss, pain, scars. You see fellow survivors who don't make it. You lie awake at night scared.

If you get past that first year, you still think about it every day. Is it back? You do breast exams in the dark feeling for some lump that you're convinced is eluding you. You don't trust your body not to turn on you again. You pray your mammograms and X-rays are clean. You hold on to your family. You make deals with God: Please give me another year, another ten years. Let me see my child grow up.

If you're lucky, like me, time goes by. And one day, you actually forget to think about breast cancer. You almost feel guilty about it. You go back to life and work without breast cancer on your mind. Therapists say it's healthy to move on, and so you do.

I've told my story of being diagnosed with breast cancer many times over the years: an aggressive tumor that didn't show up on a mammogram, a trusted doctor who told me nothing was wrong, six months of it growing bigger, close to my chest wall. I told this story publicly in 1991 in Philadelphia when few were talking about breast cancer, before all the pink ribbons.

But as time went on, it sometimes felt like I was talking about someone else. I didn't want to emotionally connect to my thirty-five-year-old self. It hurt too much.

This day was different. My friend and yoga instructor Jennifer Schelter and Living Beyond Breast Cancer asked me to go to Yoga on the Steps and say a few words to survivors. Jennifer was leading everyone on the Philadelphia Art Museum Steps.

Picture it. A thousand women putting their yoga mats side

by side on what we call the "Rocky Steps," facing the skyline of the city. That morning was a little chilly. But as Jennifer started to speak, the sun came out. Our sun salutations in unison were beautiful. Our warrior pose was powerful.

I don't remember exactly what I said, but I do remember I cried. It surprised me when I had to wipe tears from my face. I don't know why exactly. Maybe because I try so hard to put breast cancer behind me, but on this day, with these women I wasn't guarding that space in my heart. I opened up with each pose, enjoying the communal stretch. I reached back to the young mother I was when I was told I had a tumor in my right breast. I closed my eyes and remembered that feeling, like the floor was dropping beneath me and I was falling. But there I was solidly on the steps. I looked around and took comfort in the women around me. We were moving together, and in this moment we were goddesses. We were strong and powerful; a force. It was as if we willed the sun to shine on us and demand the city look at us.

It's important to honor and recognize where we've been: what we've survived and what we've accomplished. We need to remember the scars; the struggle is part of what makes us wonderfully unique and human. And then we should use that experience to go to the next stage in our lives . . . to move forward.

Other Firsts Like This to Try

◊ Go to a meditation class.

◊ Move with others in any new exercise class.

◊ Move and help others with your own story. Share it with one or many.

Join the Venice Beach Drum Circle: Day 151

There is deep wisdom within our very flesh, if we can only come to our senses and feel it.
—ELIZABETH A. BEHNKE

I had heard drums every night from the Venice Beach apartment we were renting for the week. Phil and I were there to visit our daughter, Alexa, in L.A. The sound was muffled, like a faint pulse.

"I want to go," I told Alexa.

"The sunset drum circle?"

"Yeah."

"Do you have a drum?"

"No."

I guess I'm not the only tourist who decided to take a walk on the wild side and join the famous Venice Drum Circle. On the way there, we found a Venice Beach store that had drums of every size and price range. I chose one that kind of looked more like a tambourine with a nice full sound and spent ten bucks on it.

We walked out on the sand while I lamely beat my new drum, but as we drew closer to the circle I felt intimidated. There was something otherworldly going on in there. People on the fringes were drumming and speaking out loud—to themselves, I wondered? Or was it drugs? Mental illness?

Inside the circle were some serious musicians leading the beat so loud and strong my whole body vibrated with it. There were feathers, tattoos, bongos, huge African drums, and tribal dancing in the sand.

My daughter told me to get in there.

"No."

"What do you mean no? You got a drum. You're here. Get in there!"

She was laughing. She knew I was wayyyyy outside of my comfort zone. Picture a middle-aged woman trying to ease into a mass of tie-dye, dreadlocks, and smells that took me back to the early '70s. I sat down with my drum on the outer edge, doing my best fake *Sure, I do this every day* routine. A couple of people tried to strike up a conversation with me. I don't remember any words that made any sense, though. One woman told me the circle was about "awakening the soul to ascend."

Well, I'm sure some of the drummers were high enough to "ascend." Me? I felt self-conscious, but no one was paying attention. Most people had their eyes closed. I tried to close my eyes, to feel whatever they were feeling *sans* drugs.

After a while I finally forgot myself. I let go, just beat my little drum, moved with the circle, the drums' pounding becoming a life-affirming heartbeat.

The cacophony went on long after the sun set, and Alexa and I walked off arm in arm, happy. We came. We saw. I drummed. I was moved by the sound and the strange connection to others in the circle, as if I'd plugged into an electric current taking in a different kind of energy.

I took my little drum home and it sits on my nightstand by my bed. Every now and then, when I feel the need to make some noise, I pick it up, close my eyes, and give it a few thumps. I like the idea that wherever I am, it connects right back to the circle.

◇ Go to or hold your own sunset party.

◇ Go to a park where you can jam with others, any instrument.

◇ Go to a drum lesson.

Eat at an Ethiopian Restaurant: Day 263

Tell me what you eat, I'll tell you who you are.
—ANTHELME BRILLAT-SAVARIN

Don't tell me eating isn't an adventure. I believe food can take you around the world; especially food that is so different from your normal diet that you don't even recognize what it is you're eating. To me, this is a great First.

I was warned Ethiopian food is very different. It is. Wonderfully so.

The Etho Café sits in a section of West Philadelphia that's close to several universities and just as close to some blocks you might not want to travel late at night. The restaurant is a little scruffy-looking and sits in the first floor of a row home.

My husband, Phil, and I peered into the window. We saw about ten tables with plastic tablecloths on them. They were all empty. It was around 6 p.m.

"Are you sure they're open?" Phil asked.

"I called earlier. They said they were. You wanna back out?"

Phil looked at the menu posted outside the door. "Hmmm. No. This looks interesting. We can give it a try."

We sat down and a lovely woman came out to welcome us.

"Hi. This is our first time here," I said. For some reason I felt the need to explain our presence. *Was this not the dinner hour for Ethiopians?*

"You were the one who called on the phone?"

"Right. That's me."

"Good, good. Okay."

I would be lying if I didn't tell you that I was thinking we should leave right then and there. Even as we sat there with menus, and I saw someone behind a curtain working in the kitchen, I kept wondering, *Is this a real restaurant? Did we just drop into the Twilight Zone?* Phil and I looked at each other for a signal. *Stay?*

Our waitress came back.

"So, we've never eaten Ethiopian food," I said apologetically. "We have no idea what to order. Can you tell us what we should get?"

"Of course." Our waitress was sweet but didn't talk a lot. She pointed to a few things, and we just said okay.

It wasn't long before she brought out a tray with a flat spongy bread as big as a placemat. Imagine something the consistency of a paper towel made to hold and absorb things. There were no utensils.

Turned out, I loved eating with my hands. I wish I could tell you exactly what we ate. I can't. There was some chicken thing, some really spicy thing, some egg, a meat thing, and a salad thing. We liked most of it, and left feeling quite satisfied we'd had an adventure, our palates piqued by the new tastes just fifteen minutes from our home.

Sure there's comfort in going to the same restaurants and ordering your favorite dish. But, come on. Where's the spice in your life? Food is such an easy way to go somewhere exotic without getting on a plane. Life is a big, fat exciting menu. Order up something different.

Other Firsts Like This to Try

◊ Eat at the most exotic restaurants in your area. Moroccan? Burmese? Korean barbeque?

◊ Go to a farmers' market. Look for something there to eat you've never tried before.

◊ Try a unique theme restaurant: an all-chocolate menu, all crepes, all fondue, singing waiters.

Final Thoughts

Just get up and go! You don't have to leave town to experience something that's new to you. We all have a mental list of places we mean to visit but haven't yet: the museum you've never been to, the theater in your town, a concert hall, a tourist attraction, a park. Maybe it's an annual event: a festival, a state fair, an art show or exhibit. It can be a class, a group to join, a trip to sign up for. Give anything a try once. You don't have to do it again. Just add it to your repertoire of experiences. All of it adds freshness and flavor to your life.

Push yourself to move, especially if you feel stagnant. The newness will invigorate you, taking you outside your everyday norm.

TIPS FOR FINDING FIRSTS THAT MOVE YOU

- Play tourist. Make a list of all the museums, attractions, parks, and places in your hometown you've never visited. Start going and cross them off your list.

- "What did you do over the weekend?" Have a good answer. Try to make it a point to go to one new place before you start your workweek again. Don't let your time off be a computer or TV marathon. Going one new place will help you feel more refreshed and vibrant and ready to start your workweek again.

- If you do leave town for business or pleasure, make it a point to see the sites, experience something new. Get out of your hotel. Out-of-town vacations are perfect for trying lots of new Firsts.

- What moves your soul? What stirs you inside? Move toward that. Celebrate a holiday of a different religion, go to a different church or temple, dip into a different culture or experience for your mind and heart.

CHAPTER 5

I Dare Me!

Adrenaline Rush Firsts

It's a good thing I didn't always know what I was in for when I signed up for some of my more daring Firsts.

Let's just say that if you'd explained to me that the 10k mud run for MS is a hard-core brutal obstacle course that is best attempted by twentysomethings who've trained for it with a team, I might have just taken a pass. I, however, picked up the colorful brochure at the gym and naively thought, *What a great First! Who doesn't want to crawl around in mud for a good cause?*

It was already hot as hell when I showed up alone at the Newtown Square, Pennsylvania, obstacle site in long workout pants and heavy boots (which is what was recommended). I'd tried to convince some of my friends to join me, but no one seemed as interested in trekking through mud as I was.

About a thousand people were warming up for the event. I noticed almost everyone was in a group with matching T-shirts, doing push-ups and hard-core calisthenics. *Uh-oh*, I thought. *What is this?*

I stood in the registration line next to a group of young women talking about how nervous they were about the run. *Run? I was going to take a leisurely jog.* They were all dressed in bright blue T-shirts that said Kathe's Krusaders and wore matching blue headbands. They were laughing and teasing each other. I was looking for a bathroom.

"Hi, guys. You all have any idea where the restrooms are?"

"Yeah, sure." A tall pretty blonde with a big smile turned to me. "I think up that way. You on a team?"

"No, and actually I'm really worried now. I didn't prepare. I have no idea what this is."

The girls told me they were from South Jersey. Jenna Stevens, the blonde, was their fearless leader. Her cousin Stephanie, her sister-in-law Colleen, and friends Rebecca and Melanie made up the rest of the team.

"Who is Kathe?" Looking at their shirts again.

"Oh, I named us Kathe's Krusaders," Jenna explained. "My mom, Kathe, died of MS. We're running in her honor."

I looked at this group. They were all young enough; they could have been my daughters. "I bet she would be proud of all of you."

They looked at me.

Jenna said, "Be on our team."

"What?"

"Yes," they all chimed in. "Be on our team."

"Look, guys, that's really nice, but I'm fifty-three years old, and I don't know if I'm going to be able to keep up with you."

"You'll be fine. We're not going to go fast."

"Really?? That's great. Okay. Thank you. Thank you for adopting me."

I had known them for a minute, and yet this felt absolutely right. Kathe's Krusaders took me in. They now had a motherly mascot. I lined up with them at the start. A siren went off and we were moving.

The first mile was pretty easy: A little jog through the woods, over some logs and a dip into a muddy lake. No problem. The water was a refreshing initiation.

"Let's get down and dirty!" Jenna yelled. It didn't take any time to see she was spunky, outgoing. The team psyched to follow her lead. "Whoo hoo!" We all went in with clean clothes . . . we all came out with a beautiful shiny coat of mud on us. Now I looked more like one of Kathe's Krusaders.

We jogged some more. The sun baked the mud on our face, chest, arms, and shoes, making the run a little tougher before we got to the next obstacle. It was almost a relief to get down on our hands and knees and wallow through a slimy creek bed under ropes. We were a sight. Spectators were laughing and cheering us on.

I was having a good time. I felt a huge adrenaline rush keeping up with the girls.

But the next challenge was a real obstacle. You had to balance and walk across a twelve-foot-long log hanging over a six-foot-deep gulley to get to the other side. The girls did this easily. I cheered them on. *Go Jenna. You got this Stephanie!* But when it was my turn, I froze. I wanted to go. My head said no.

"You guys go on!" I hollered.

"No!" Jenna shouted. "We're not going without you."

Oh darn. Okay, I thought, *I have no choice.*

I panicked and went for plan B. I lay down on the log and inched my way across like an inchworm with my big tush in the air. It was painful. It was slow. I was holding up the line. Kathe's Krusaders did not budge. "You got this, Lu Ann!" "Yahoo . . . ride that log!"

I thought, *I so love these women.* They stood on the other side, hands out, pulling me up to my feet as soon as they could reach me and we were running again . . . laughing.

"Thank you. My heroes! You sure you want me on this team?"

"Ha-ha. Absolutely."

I'd brought a flip cam with me and we all passed it around, taking video, trying to keep the mud from mucking it up.

I focused the camera on the obstacle up ahead: a twenty-by-twenty-foot wall of rope ladders. You had to scale the wall as it jiggled around, throw your body over the top of the metal frame, and ease your way down. Colleen is short, about my size. I watched her tackle it first. She had to stretch her whole body to throw one foot up; she'd get her balance then pull herself up to the next level, planting her foot on another rope step.

I was determined not to slow the team down. I attacked the ropes. I did just what Colleen did. I didn't think about it until I got to the top. I heard their voices. *"You can do it, Lu Ann. Throw your leg over the top!"* I took a deep breath and then . . . I just did it.

The girls whooped and hollered. With every obstacle I felt stronger and more a part of this team.

Along the way, I learned about the women who had been complete strangers to me at the beginning of this race. I found out Jenna was a schoolteacher for special needs kids, Colleen was trying to get pregnant, Melinda had a boyfriend, Stephanie was trying to quit smoking, and Rebecca was planning her wedding.

By the end, the mud was sliding into my boots and I was having trouble running. I tried to slow down, but the girls grabbed my hands like we were in the *Wizard of Oz* about to enter the Emerald City. But we weren't skipping through a field of poppies. We were slogging through a field of mud, then climbing up a steep hill to a big earthen slide. We sat down, raised our arms in unison, screaming all the way down on our butts until we splashed together in a deep muddy lake.

You had to swim and scramble out to the other side, crawl up the bank on hands and knees under more ropes, and make one more final run to the finish line. I think Kathe's Krusaders literally dragged me, laughing, cheering, "Almost, almost, stay together . . ." all the way to the end where we collapsed, high-fived, and gave each other big muddy hugs.

We stood together as firemen sprayed us down with hoses to get some of the mud off of us. We were done, sopping wet now, but I didn't want to say good-bye. I was in awe of these women.

Why did they bring me along? What possessed Jenna to pull me in? I never asked her. But I know I was thinking about her mother, Kathe. I thought, *You did a fine job. This is one brave, passionate daughter you have here with wonderful friends. Are you with us today?* I was honored to be a Krusader.

I walked away feeling alive and unstoppable. *If I could climb walls and crawl through mud*, I thought, *then there's nothing that I can't conquer with determination and perseverance. Nothing.*

The mud run put gas in my tank. It refueled me. At home, at work, in everything I did, the experience gave me such a jolt of confidence. It was so beyond what I'd ever attempted before physically.

The thing is, you can't feel this way unless you take some chances, unless you surprise yourself, do something that is beyond your everyday experience. You have to seek it out, look for it, push yourself, be willing to fall on your face, or look silly.

I was a screaming mess when I rode a mechanical bull, and I was completely unprepared for roller derby. Zip lining was nerve-wracking. Laser tag was a blast, and what a hoot to swing from a trapeze. Every one of these Firsts woke me up, challenged my senses and my spirit.

Any contest, any game, any race, anything that brings you fully energized into the moment and leaves you with an endorphin high will be an emotional lifter. These Firsts require an "I dare me" attitude. Get through it and the psychological rewards are great. Share the experience with others? Even better.

I knew the three-hour gritty mud run was a real once-in-a-lifetime First with Jenna and Kathe's Krusaders. Jenna wasn't just honoring her mom. All of us on her team were inspired, honoring our own lives by living them passionately, pushing ourselves to give our best right to the finish line.

Ride Zip Lines and Rappel into Cenote: Day 71

It is not down in any map; true places never are.
—HERMAN MELVILLE

EVIDENCE ADRENALINE RUSH FIRSTS CAN BENEFIT YOU

- It's the feel-good endorphins. Endorphins are peptides produced by the pituitary gland and the hypothalamus in the brain. Scientists say they're released in the body during exercise, excitement, pain, and sex. They resemble opiates to produce a feeling of well-being.

- Michael Gass, at the University of New Hampshire, says his studies show risk-taking experiences increase confidence, and the learning from those events transfers to other life situations.

- A study published by the *Journal of Personality and Social Psychology* shows 57 percent of the participants were happier after spending money on an experience, instead of something material.

There are zip lines and then there are crazy zip lines. I didn't know this until I went to Mexico on vacation.

I'd never been to Mexico before, but I'd already warned my husband, Phil, who can be perfectly content sitting on the beach, that I was in First mode and looking for big vacation adventures.

Our vacation consultant at our hotel in Playa del Carmen was more than happy to accommodate.

"How about a Mayan Zip Line Adventure?" he suggested.

"Sí. Muy bien." I nodded to our consultant. "Excelente."

A couple of days before, he'd sent us to a nature amusement park called Xplor. Phil and I experienced our First zip line adventure there. We were strapped into brand-new harnesses by employees going through multiple safety checks before we whooshed high above the park on wires strung from tall man-made towers. After a day of zipping, we wanted more, so the Mayan adventure sounded perfect. We had no idea what we'd signed up for.

We got off a tour bus and started trekking through the jungle to get to a Mayan village. Our Indiana Jones–type guide was using a machete to clear a path while warning us, "If you see this plant, don't touch it. It will kill you." I turned to Phil and said, "We're not in Disneyland anymore." I wondered if I read all the fine print on the paperwork we signed. "Did we release responsibility in case of death on this?"

Our group included a couple of families from Memphis, Tennessee, with young kids. The parents were all doctors. Something about that made me feel better, but then I saw the zip line we'd be using. Unlike our Xplor visit, this apparatus looked like it was fifty years old. We weren't zipping between man-made towers; we were zipping from tree to tree, just a step beyond swinging vines, in the jungle, over a crocodile-infested lake. We were all handed big wooden sticks to use as our brake when we got to the other side. The sticks had a crudely carved hook on it. You had to pull that hook down on the wire to stop or you might go flying into a tree.

"Do you remember seeing this in the brochure?" I asked Phil.

"Nope. But, you wanted adventure. You got it." I could tell he was amused by the fact that I'd finally gotten myself into a First I wasn't sure I could handle. He, of course, embraced it and went first. I watched him throw his stick up at the end of the wire and stop himself. He looked like a crazy Tarzan. He motioned for me to cross over. "You come, Jane." I laughed. I looked down at the lake. "Hi, crocodile. Hope you aren't waiting for a big dinner."

I checked my rusty, well-used harness, gripped my big brake stick, and took a leap. The zip was only about thirty seconds, but it felt longer. I held my breath, waited for a signal, then used my "brake." Ha. It worked. *Wow.* I thought, *That was pretty exciting. I did it.*

I watched the rest of the group go across without incident. Everybody felt pretty high after getting past that obstacle, and we bonded through the rest of this too-real experience we'd been thrown in together.

We rappelled fifty feet into a cenote, an underground cave. We climbed the steps of the ancient Mayan ruin in Coba, which was like the Rocky steps times ten. We visited with a Mayan shaman for a traditional ceremony. We ate a rustic homemade lunch in a Mayan village that probably would not have passed USDA approval. I walked through a Mayan home with a dirt floor and watched a child play in the yard with a wild monkey.

I have to tell you, I don't think there is an American tourist company that would ever risk such a wild, raw adventure. I have no idea what the procedure would be if someone got hurt. It wasn't Disneyworld. But it was glorious. All my senses were on hyperdrive, taking in every nuance of this jungle tour. At the end of the day, Phil and I felt like we'd gone "off the map" into uncharted territory. It bonded us in an intoxicatingly risky little adventure. I'd do it again in a racing heartbeat.

◇ Wherever you go on vacation, challenge yourself. If you can, go on tours that are a little physically challenging. Get off the beaten trail.

◇ Try white water rafting.

◇ Go for a hike up a mountain or trail.

◇ Rent Rollerblades, a moped, or a Segway.

Swing on the Trapeze: Day 144

Any workout which does not involve a certain minimum of danger or responsibility does not improve the body—it just wears it out.
—NORMAN MAILER

I was never a big fan of the circus, except for one part: the trapeze act. I was dazzled by those strong-armed guys catching beautiful women doing gymnastics in the air, terrified they'd miss and fall into the net below.

I had no net under me when I attempted to do my own trapeze act at the Philadelphia School of Circus Arts. Instead, there was a big fat mattress below. All I could think was *Please don't let me fall.*

Niff Nichols was my "flight instructor." She is one tough trapeze chick. I had no idea how much physical strength it takes to just get up on the round wooden bar swing suspended by ropes from the ceiling. But of course Niff made everything look easy. She glided up on the trapeze, gracefully flipping over the bar, standing on it, striking a pose. She's a small girl but all muscle built from years of trapeze work.

I think I'm in relatively good shape for my age. I lift some weights. I do cardio. But when Niff asked me to hoist myself up on the swing, it wasn't happening. I had to jump while she gave me a boost to the bar. That was the easy part.

Niff instructed me to hang by my legs and then pull myself up to a standing position. "What?!"

My little muscles were crying. The bar was swinging unsteadily with every move.

"Pull! Do it! You can!"

I could tell Niff had lots of experience with people like me who think they're fit, only to find out they aren't fit enough to be the circus clown. Somehow I got there. Somehow I was standing on the trapeze bar, high above the mattress.

I was shaking but I was also excited. "High heels!" Niff was shouting from below for me to lift onto my toes on the bar. "High heels!" Right.

I looked down. "Don't look down!" Right.

The adrenaline was flowing. My hands were sweating on the ropes. Not a good thing.

"Okay now. Lift one leg off the bar."

"What?"

"You can do it. Lift one leg, bend the knee, point your toe and bring it to your other knee and throw your body forward, your arms behind you, still holding on to the rope and pose!"

I stopped questioning and just tried to do what Niff said. And there it was, my flying trapeze pose, the one I'd seen at the circus so many times as the crowd went wild applauding with amazement. WHOA!

My heart was pounding, excited. This was nuts. Fabulous and nuts.

"Okay," I said. "This is great. How do I get down?"

It turns out, down is harder than up when you're on a trapeze. These are things you don't think about before you sign up for circus class. I'm just warning you.

"Slowly pull back, kick one leg out, and ease your butt down to the bar."

"AHHHHHH."

"You got this. Butt to the bar."

My butt, my legs, my everything were in muscle-spasming shock.

"Now hang by your legs. Pull one leg off the bar. Look at what you're doing."

I don't remember what happened next. Somehow I stuck a landing on the firm mattress below my feet.

Oh yeah! It was one of the coolest things I've ever done. I bow down to trapeze artists with renewed appreciation.

Obviously, I won't be running away to the circus. Still, I appreciated a strong, confident coach was able to push me beyond my normal limits. She believed I could do it, and so I did. Sometimes we need a coach who can get us there; lift us past our own fears to help us fly to new heights in our experience.

◇ Take a hot air balloon ride or helicopter ride.

◇ Get ready for a medieval duel. Take a fencing lesson.

◇ Learn to climb a rope.

Ride a Mechanical Bull: Day 232

I have accepted fear as a part of life—specifically the fear of change. . . . I have gone ahead despite the pounding in the heart that says: turn back.

    —ERICA JONG

One day, during my Year of Firsts, my daughter, Alexa, who was following my blog from L.A, called me and said, "I don't think some of these Firsts are exciting enough."

"Really," I'd responded sarcastically. "Well, since you're so critical, feel free to schedule something 'exciting' for me."

And she did. That's how I ended up on a mechanical bull!

"I'm going to do what?"

"I found a mechanical bull for you to ride. Just go to the Buckhead Bar in Philly, and they'll be waiting for you after you're done with work."

I could hear her trying to stifle a giggle on the phone as she told me.

"What if your old mom hurts herself, huh?"

"Call 9-1-1."

I wasn't sure I was in the right place. The bar was dark and empty. It was a weeknight. I guess the drinking crowd wasn't out yet. I walked to the back and spotted the bull. I'd imagined this was going to be just a step above a mechanical pony ride. But this "bull" was on-steroids huge and stood in the middle of something like a gigantic inflatable bed.

I found the bull operator, a young guy who clearly questioned my sanity. I mean how many middle-aged women walk into a bar by themselves and say, "Let me ride the bull"?

"You ever been on one of these things before?" He looked worried.

"Listen, this was my daughter's idea. I'm doing this for a blog. Every day I do something I've never done before. Today, I'm riding this thing."

"Right, okay then, get up there."

I bounced around on the air-cushioned pillow and hoisted myself up.

"What do I hold on to?"

"Scoot forward and hold on to the strap on the saddle."

The bull started to pitch forward, and that's when the high-pitched girly screams began. Have you ever been on a roller coaster that you wanted to get off of but you couldn't, where you weren't sure if you were going to lose your lunch or cry? Same experience here.

The guys working in the bar had no idea I wanted off. They were having a pretty good laugh watching me; my upper body being whipped around. I looked like some crazy bull-riding mama.

Words weren't coming out of my mouth, just "the scream." You'd think I'd just let go and fall, but I was terrified to do that.

Instead, I held on like my life depended on it. The bull operator couldn't shake me off. The scream continued.

The bull vibrated, violently moving back and forth, pitching this way and that. My palms were sweating, holding on to the saddle strap with a death grip. The scream never stopped.

After what seemed like an eternity and the operator put the bull in its highest bucking gear, the thing finally threw me loose, tossing me into the air. I felt my body brace for the impact I dreaded, still screaming.

There was a loud *plop*, as I made a surprisingly soft landing on the surrounding air bed.

No more scream. Just silence. I didn't move.

"You okay?" the operator said.

My heart was still pounding. I kind of checked myself to see if I was all in one piece. Finally, I laughed, "Yeah, I'm okay."

I tried to stand up. "I don't even know what to say about that. That's quite a ride. Not sure I would do that again, though."

The operator chuckled. "You held on pretty long. Gotta hand it to you."

"I guess that's what happens when adrenaline kicks in. I couldn't let go."

It was a good cheap thrill, and I have to admit, the video is hysterical.

Sometimes my daughter will say, "Need a laugh?"

"Yep."

"Mechanical bull video?"

"Yep."

Then we hold our sides watching it. It works every time.

Not only does the video remind me to laugh at myself, but in a very literal way it shows me sometimes it's okay to let go. I usually hold on to things because I'm afraid of what comes next . . . the unknown. When I watch that video, I see myself flying off that mechanical bull and know it's all right to be thrown and tossed into the air now and then—I can still land safely.

But after the bull, I did decide to schedule my own thrilling Firsts from that point on.

Other Firsts Like This to Try

◊ Get on a new roller coaster ride.

◊ Take a rock climbing and rappelling class.

◊ Jump off the high dive.

Play Laser Tag: Day 242

There is no pleasure worth forgoing just for an extra three years in the geriatric ward.
—JOHN MORTIMER

I really did try to convince some friends to come play laser tag with me.

"A First?"

"Yeah, come on, it will be fun."

They just rolled their eyes at me. Keep in mind my friends are in their fifties. They think they're too old for this stuff. It's a shame because nothing makes you feel younger than a good adrenaline rush.

I went on my own. However, this proved to be a problem when I got to Grand Slam USA in Malvern, Pennsylvania. You have to have at least one other person to shoot at to play laser tag. I got some questioning looks from the high school teens running the operation that day. I'm sure they aren't used to seeing a "mom" type come in without kids in tow.

I was just about to give up on the idea when a family came in. Allie, who was probably about ten, brought her parents in to play. A couple of the guys in the game center decided they'd help fill out our group so we could do "boys against girls." *Awesome.*

They took us into a room to get our space age–looking computerized lime green laser body vests. I felt like Barbarella. (See Jane Fonda in her first big movie.) They handed us big laser guns that looked like galactic war weapons.

Allie was more than happy to share the secrets of laser tag with me.

"Look for the disco ball. After a while you have to recharge your laser gun."

"In the middle of battle?"

"Yeah, don't worry. I'll show you."

It was Allie's mom's first time too. She just shrugged her shoulders, and we followed her daughter's confident lead.

We walked through a game arena that was clearly meant to be a flashback to the '70s. There were glow paint murals on a maze of black walls, and when the lights went out, I had a feeling I was walking through some "bad trip."

My heart started racing.

"Hide!" Allie said in a loud whisper.

All of a sudden I heard *pyew, pyew, pyew* . . . Laser firings.

"Am I hit?" I wasn't sure. My gun wouldn't fire. I kept pulling the trigger. Then it worked. Some shadow was coming toward me with a blinking light. FIRE FIRE FIRE . . .

"You got him," Allie said, coming up behind me.

"I did?"

"Recharge your laser now."

A surprise attack from Allie's dad and the boys took us off guard. We ran blindly through the maze, down dark paths, not knowing where they went. We launched an offensive attack from a second floor. It was a nice try, but apparently too late. GAME OVER!

"What? What do you mean game over? I just got started."

Everyone was laughing. In our ten-minute game, the boys had smoked us good.

I had to thank Allie for being my laser tag guide. Her passion and willingness to share her "inside knowledge" made it that much more fun for the rest of us. And once again, in a place where I was alone, wanting to try something new, I was "adopted" as we shared a heart-pumping experience.

Don't be afraid to go after your adrenaline rush First solo. If you're open, you'll find you won't be alone for long.

And for my next birthday party? I want laser tag.

Other Firsts Like This to Try

◊ Play paintball.

◊ Ride go-karts.

◊ Do a corn maze.

Audition for Roller Derby: Day 319

Panic at the thought of doing a thing is a challenge to do it.
—HENRY S. HASKINS

I can't really roller-skate, so that was issue number one. Still, I thought, why should that stop me from auditioning for the baddest girl roller derby team on the planet? Who doesn't want to put their princess tiara down and smoothly slink around a roller rink in heavy knee pads and a helmet, looking like you could kick anyone's behind who dares look at you sideways?

I'd seen video of the Philly Roller Girls. They are some seriously tough chicks. When I saw they were having auditions, I had a crazy fantasy of being able to roll with them. You know, to be scrappy enough to rumble in the rink. Okay, I'd never actually seen a game in person, but I did see the movie *Kansas City Bomber* with Raquel Welch.

I tried to channel Raquel when I got to the rink in Camden, New Jersey. Women of every age and size stood in line registering to audition. When I wrote my name on the audition list, someone laughed and said, "We could call you Wrath of Cahn." I have been called that at work before, and it wasn't necessarily a compliment. I just tried to think positive; maybe "I Cahn do it."

A woman who called herself R2Dcup skated by me then turned back around to ask me if I had my own gear for the audition.

"Nope. I'm gearless."

"No, problem." She handed me a helmet with the name *Wicked* painted on it.

"Cool. Thanks."

I put on some very used roller derby skates and a bunch of big fat pads on my knees and elbows, took tiny baby roller steps to the rink, and held on to the side wall with the other "girls" to wait for my turn to "show my stuff."

Now I was nervous. Maybe this wasn't such a good idea. Maybe I was going to hurt myself here. I noticed some beautiful athletic women in this crowd. One stunner towering over me told me she was an interior designer.

"Why do you want to do this?" I asked.

"I don't know. Always wanted to."

She didn't ask me why I wanted to do this. I'm sure she quickly sized me up as some nutty broad who would be no threat to her. I realized I just wanted to get through an audition without breaking any bones.

A Philly Roller Girl who looked like she could live up to her name, "Mo Pain," told me they had an anesthesiologist on the team. I guess that makes sense. I imagined them speeding around the rink elbowing, brawling, getting into hair-pulling, wrestling kind of fights during a game. You need someone on the team to knock people out.

Mo Pain got into the middle of the track and explained the first round of auditions.

"We want to see you do a crossover move, pick up some speed, and then skate on one leg . . . if we like what we see, you'll move on to round two."

I was nervous. I tried to practice the moves they wanted to

see, but I skated like I did at a fourth-grade birthday party, tee-tering back and forth and threatening to make a fabulous fall one way or the other.

I watched other women easily glide around the track, cross-ing each leg smoothly over the other as they rounded the cor-ners. They picked one leg up, balancing effortlessly on the other skate.

I did think about backing out. My heart was pounding. I'm sure the women around me were wondering why someone who could be their mom and was holding the wall would be audi-tioning. Instead, I tried to explain myself, as I often do when I know I'm way over my head. "I just want to survive. I'm doing this for a first-time experience."

"Oh wow," they said. They were more than appreciative of my mission. When I tentatively rolled into the rink, they gave me moral support, clapping and whooping.

I made my way slowly around the track, nearly tripped but held on to my balance as I attempted but didn't complete a crossover.

"That's okay. That's okay. You can do it," I heard from the crowd.

I picked up one leg for half a second and got big props; the crowed whistled and stomped. I laughed, which nearly did me in. I got through a lap. I wouldn't call it a victory lap. I would call it a roller derby clown act; you know, something that made everyone in there with real skating skills feel a little better about their chances of making the team.

I didn't get to tangle with anyone or make it to round two. I gave back my Wicked helmet feeling fine that I just added a little sweat inside it.

◊ Audition for any sports team, even if you know there's no way you'll make the cut.

◊ Try ice hockey, tag football, snowboarding, or boxing.

◊ Join a bowling league.

Final Thoughts

You don't have to jump out of a plane or cliff dive to get a life-affirming adrenaline rush. Still, you have to take some risks that challenge you physically or mentally. Think about something you've always wanted to do but never pushed yourself to follow through. Did you always want to get into a race car, go ocean kayaking, run your first 5k, or learn to surf or skateboard?

When we're stuck, we often play it safe; maybe too safe. Every day we put on seat belts, we lock our doors, we don't talk to strangers. These are all good things to do. But mentally, every once in a while, we need to "hang it all out there," attempt an exhilarating feat, really live our dreams.

It's easy to make excuses: "can't," "too old," "will fail," "will look stupid." We all have weaknesses and disabilities. If you have a bad back, you should not get on a mechanical bull. Still, we don't push the limits of what is possible. You may think you are protecting yourself by staying safely at home, but in fact the real fountain of youth is in the "doing," in the places where the unexpected happens, and in a life where you say "I dare me."

TIPS FOR FINDING "I DARE ME" FIRSTS

- What would you do if you could summon the courage? If it's a challenge that seems insurmountable, break it down into steps. Want to go scuba diving? First sign up for a class at your local Y. Take small steps to give you confidence and training to get to your big moment.

- Expand your friendships. There are clubs for everything. If you want to learn to rock climb or hike or ski, join a club that encourages and supports that adrenaline rush dream you have.

- Make chores a game. Put a stopwatch on the mundane cleaning or shopping. Race your kids or your friends and get your heart pumping with the competition.

- Follow the leader. Let the kids in your life pick the adrenaline rush adventure (within reason). Sometimes watching them jump off the high dive can be the inspiration for us to take a brave jump too!

CHAPTER 6

Firsts in Class

Learning Firsts

"What do you mean I have to take the Graduate Record Exam?"

I was trying to get into the University of Missouri Online Journalism Master's Program. This was six months before I started my Year of Firsts, and my head was not in a good place.

"Seriously?" I vented to the admissions person on the phone. "I am fifty-two years old and have over thirty years of journalism experience, and you are going to make me take the GRE?" (I might have also said, "I'm a national investigative Emmy Award winner. . . .")

The woman talking to me from Mizzou was not impressed. She said those were the rules, and they didn't let Pulitzer Prize winners into the program either unless they take the test and make a decent score. *AHHHHHHHH!* I knew the GRE was half math—all the math I loathed in high school and long ago forgot.

"Why do I have to add mixed fractions, and calculate the volume of a cube just to go back to school?" I whined.

I'd always thought I'd eventually get my master's so I could teach. As the economy tanked and colleagues were losing their jobs, I figured this was a good time to beef up my skills and resume. Mizzou had one of the few programs in the country that I could fit into my full-time schedule with work. But Mizzou wasn't going to make it easy.

I bought some GRE practice books just to see what my addled brain was up against. It was 2009. I hadn't been in school since 1978. One look at the algebra, geometry, and word problems sent me into a meltdown. I slammed the practice books shut and sulked. I complained to anyone who listened. Instead of figuring out how to take the GRE, I tried to figure out some way I could appeal to a reasonable person at the school to let me in sans test.

Finally, my husband, Phil, said, "Enough already. Are you going to talk about this, or are you going to do it? Take the test!"

Don't you just hate when your significant other nails it on the head and makes you look at your pathetic self? I knew he was right. I just had to get past the test, so I hired a tutor.

Let me just say the mental effort it took to study for the GRE was like trying to start a car that had been sitting idle in the driveway for years. It took a while before that ancient part of my brain used for math sputtered, kicked over, and started running again. But when it did, I knew something good was happening. The lights came back on. I woke up.

As if it wasn't humbling enough to have to hire someone to help me get through the math section, I had to take the GRE twice. But finally, I passed Mizzou's standards, and the school graciously opened their online doors to me.

I did a happy dance. My family patted me on the back. For the first time in a long time, I realized I was pleased with myself: I'd taken on a difficult challenge outside my comfort zone, and it felt wonderful to have persisted and worked through it.

Looking back, I believe it was the act of learning again that helped me figure out how to get my life back on track. The idea of doing Firsts came into my brain because I actually started *using* my brain again. I was sweeping away some of the cobwebs in that "upstairs attic" and making room for some new fresh positive thinking. It was a first step.

I officially started school in the first weeks of my Year of Firsts. But much of the real learning happened outside of my academic pursuits. The Year of Firsts was my life classroom.

I took a smorgasbord of classes and lessons as Firsts. I learned to bake a cake from scratch and how to roll sushi. I tried all sorts of dancing lessons. I learned to swing a golf club. I took a drum lesson. I went to an art class. I learned how to knit, use a sewing machine, blow glass, make mosaics. I took any kind of new exercise class I could find. I learned the rules of hockey from an intern. I learned how to tell a joke and do a magic trick. I challenged myself to learn how to use every new social media and technology tool I could.

I failed miserably at a lot of this stuff, but it didn't matter. I enjoyed trying, taking in new information. I was on a "learning high."

It wasn't that I wasn't using my brain all these previous years. But let's face it: As adults, we get proficient at what we do (hopefully). We lean on all of our experience and habits, and that's fine and good. But when it becomes rote, we can get stuck. And in my case, when the world was changing around me, I was so entrenched and married to my usual ways of thinking and doing, I didn't want to budge. I was turned off to learning and growing.

Eventually, I found that even some of the silliest memory exercises, like learning the alphabet backwards, were Firsts that lit up some new pathway in my brain.

As of this writing, I'm still working on getting my master's degree. I take classes as I can work them into my crazy schedule. I can tell you, for me, every class is a lot of work. Sometimes, getting my brain wrapped around a class like "qualitative research methods" is like trudging through mud. But, when I eventually get this degree, I know I will have earned it.

I should really write Mizzou a thank-you note for not rolling over when I asked for a pass on their test. They tested me all right. They tested my commitment to learning and made me prove something to myself: that I was willing and wanted to be a lifelong learner. And that paved the way for one of the most incredible years of my life.

Learn the Alphabet Backwards: Day 5

A person who never made a mistake never tried anything new.
—ALBERT EINSTEIN

They say the brain starts a steady downward decline in your fifties. No kidding. I can attest to the fact: Some days I suddenly

SCIENTIFIC EVIDENCE LEARNING FIRSTS WILL IMPROVE YOUR LIFE

- Numerous studies show learning spurs the growth of new brain cells. But the chair of Neurosurgery at Cedars-Sinai Medical Center in Los Angeles, Keith L. Black, MD, says, "It's not enough to do the things you routinely do—like the daily crossword. You have to learn new things, like Sudoku or a new form of bridge."

- Research shows learning any new physical activity may be the best way to keep your brain young. Professor Art Kramer at the University of Illinois says high exercise levels can reduce the risk of dementia by 30 to 40 percent.

- Research at Brandeis University shows education appears to slow the brain's aging process. A college degree can take ten years off your brain age and may help you live longer. Continuing education will do the same thing.

can't remember a coworker's name or how to spell a common word or where I left my keys or even where I parked my car.

I like to attribute this to what we in the business call "News-heimers." It means our brains are so full of news facts we can't remember the simple stuff. Unfortunately, I have to admit I feel pretty sure it's more than "Newsheimers" and I've lost some brain cells in the last decade.

I believe all the experts who say you might not lose your marbles if you keep testing and challenging your brain with new puzzles and problems. Still, I didn't think learning the alphabet backwards would be that challenging.

"Can you do it?" I asked my work partner/photographer Dave Bentley. We were in a news car on the way to shoot a story.

"Sure." I turned my flip cam on and sure enough, I took video of him fluidly, without effort, reciting the alphabet backwards while driving.

"Zyxwvutsrqponmlkjihgfedcba."

"How do you do that?"

"Just a talent."

"You didn't even look at it. You think I can do it?"

"No," he said smugly. His brain is about a decade younger. Unfair competition.

I start, "Z, y . . . uh . . . x . . . hmmm . . . ugh."

Dave reminded me I left my purse in a bathroom the day before and it took me a while to remember where it was so I could retrieve it. I'd also panicked looking for my phone when it was in my hand. Seriously. Not good.

That day, I wrote out the alphabet backwards, practicing in between interviews and shoots we were doing.

By the end of the day I had it, kind of. I went home and turned on the flip cam to document my progress. It took me a couple of tries but I finally, painstakingly, spit it out.

The next day Dave asked me if I could recite the alphabet backwards.

"Sure, smarty pants. I've got this. Zyxwvutsrqponmlkjihg-fedcab."

"C-a-b??"

"I mean a-b-c, uh, c-b-a. Whatever!!"

Yeah, I know. Silly, right? But when was the last time you committed something new to memory? "Four score and seven years ago . . ." In seventh grade maybe? We have so many phone numbers on speed dial, you don't even have to memorize your home phone number anymore. (Don't ask me what mine is.)

The point is, researchers say testing your brain like this is not dumb. It's like giving your brain a little pop quiz—just a little something to keep you sharper, longer. And it's an easy First.

Other Firsts Like This to Try

◊ Try the *New York Times* Sunday crossword puzzle. Keep at it and see if you can improve every week.

◊ Learn the lineup of your local baseball or football team. (Okay, it was challenging for me.)

◊ Learn how to do Sudoku or the Jumble in the paper.

Soul Line Dancing: Day 241

Don't think. Just Dance.
  —ALEXA HOUSER (MY DAUGHTER)

My daughter loves to dance. She thinks it's the most freeing, nonthinking escape in the world. But experts believe it may actually be the best "thinking" thing you can do. Apparently, any kind of dance in which you have to learn steps is a perfect combination of exercise and food for your brain.

I considered this excellent news during my Year of Firsts, as I attempted almost any kind of dance class I could find. Okay, I didn't make it to Pole Dancing. (It's on my to-do list.) Soul line dancing turned out to be my surprise favorite.

When dance instructor Kenny Johnson heard I was looking for first-time experiences, he immediately sent me an invitation to come to one of his Soul Line Dancing Classes.

"Is this kind of like country music line dancing?"

"Yeah, but with a whole lot of *soul*."

I wasn't exactly sure what that meant when I drove to Claymont, Delaware, for Kenny's Dancing Convention. But as soon as I walked into the packed hotel ballroom I knew I'd walked into a whole lot of fun.

About three hundred people were moving in unison dancing to a funky beat and had big smiles plastered on their faces. Someone on stage was calling out steps. "Bump it right, bump it left, now turn . . ." A group of women on the edge of the dance class pulled me in to join them. "Get on in here, baby!"

Boy, were they sorry. For the first few minutes I just kept bumping the wrong way and stepping on their toes as I tried to figure out how to move and groove.

You couldn't stop paying attention for a minute or you were going to be left behind or trampled. As soon I conquered "the Chicago" step, the group leader moved on to the "shoulder roll." I desperately tried to mimic whoever was in front and to the side of me. Finally, I put a few moves together and found myself with a silly grin on my face too.

Apparently, I had not jumped into a beginner's class. When I got lost and turned around, everyone just kind of pushed me in the right direction and gave me encouragement to keep moving.

"Girl, you need some remedial soul line dancing training!" one of the ladies teased me as I shuffled the wrong way.

"You think?" I laughed.

All those grooving soul moves eventually got a little too complicated for me and I had to step aside to watch, but that was a blast too.

Maybe my daughter is right. At some point you have to not think so much, and instead just dance. Find your own style. You don't need a partner to take a class. Do what I did; try lots of different kinds of dancing. Don't wait for an invitation. People who dance are always happy to share the steps and the joy of the experience.

Other Firsts Like This to Try

◊ Try the Latin dance exercise class Zumba.

◊ Take a ballroom dance class.

◊ Try an adult tap dance class.

Take an Art Class with a Nude Model: Day 244

A man paints with his brains and not with his hands.
—MICHELANGELO

I've always wished I had some artistic talent, but I can't draw a straight line. It's so bad that if I'm with a group playing Pictionary, no one wants to be my partner. Even I can't recognize what I'm drawing.

I tell you this so you can understand how completely intimidated and nervous I was to walk into a real art studio in Center City Philadelphia for a nude sketch session. (I mean, there was a nude model there; all artists had their clothes on.) You get the picture.

Mark Bullen is a well-known portrait artist who runs the class. Artists chip in $10 each to pay the model.

When I got there, I was invited to sit among the artists in a semicircle of chairs. A young woman walked in front of us in a robe and let it drop. I think I wanted to gasp, but held my breath. I've only seen women stand naked in strip clubs (don't ask me why I was there). And once I covered a story on the set of a porn film (very bizarre). But here, everyone acted like a bowl of fruit had just been presented to them. The only sound in the room was pencil on paper.

Mark loaned me some charcoal pencils, and I opened a new sketch pad. This lovely, slender, naked young model struck a pose with her back to us, an arm extended behind her head, her face turned just slightly. All the artists around me were working quickly. They would get just ten minutes before the pose changed.

I, on the other hand, just stared. I stared at her. I stared at my blank page. My brain had no idea where to begin. Mark could see how lost I was and quietly came over, moving my hand holding the charcoal to make a couple of lines; marking where to start the head, where to put the feet.

My brain was trying to look at the body in parts. I told myself to just move my pencil in a way that would not produce a third-grade stick figure.

I tentatively started drawing a form. The guide lines Mark put on paper for me actually helped. Lo and behold, something that looked more human than alien started to appear. I watched the others shading their sketches. I tried shading too. I stopped thinking about the naked woman and looked at the light on her back. *How do you get that on paper?* The curve of her arm, a complete mystery. I quickly erased several attempted arms. Okay, my nude was going to be armless, you know, like one of those armless Greek statues. Feet kind of disappeared too because the feet I drew looked like dog paws.

Mark came by and looked at what I had. He kind of gave it a "Hmmm. Okay." He showed me with just a few quick flicks of the pencil how my drawing could take a real shape.

At the end of the hour of sketching, I felt strangely at peace, relaxed. There were no phones or beeping devices allowed in the room. The experience was so cerebral and unique that it completely took me into another world.

I did, however, leave knowing I have no current artistic talent. No matter. I learned a little bit about art and the human form and realized life is like art, isn't it? We should be creating something new all the time. It doesn't have to be a masterpiece every day, but we should be aware it's our creation, in our hands. It takes some effort, some trial and error, to be good. Firsts are a way we can draw something new on the page every day until we find something we like.

Other Firsts Like This to Try

◊ Be a nude model for an art class. (Ha, I dare ya.)

◊ Try a sculpting, pastels, or oil painting class.

◊ Take a jewelry-making or craft class.

Teach Grad School: Day 265

The dream begins with a teacher who believes in you, who tugs and pushes and leads you to the next plateau, sometimes poking you with a sharp stick called "truth."

—DAN RATHER

Sometimes when you put a desire out into the world, the world comes back with an opportunity. This is what happened when I was asked to teach investigative reporting to graduate students at Drexel University. Teaching was a dream of mine. I had no idea how much I was about to learn.

I had embarked on Firsts so that I could get "unstuck" in my life. I didn't care so much if I was good or bad at whatever I tried. It only mattered that I tried. But this First mattered. I wanted to be the same kind of teacher who inspired and motivated me when I was in school. So, of course, I was terrified when I walked into my First class.

"What makes investigative news stories different from other news stories?" I asked the class.

Eighteen faces stared at me. I thought I was used to working an audience, but not like this. I had three hours to fill on a Tuesday night. Most of my students were working full-time, like me, trying to get their master's degree in their spare time, like me. And we all knew, outside of being a guest lecturer, I'd never taught a class like this before.

I'd tried to prepare. My guide was Professor Ron Bishop. He showed me a twenty-page syllabus he'd used for the class and a choice of textbooks. I was overwhelmed. It wasn't enough to bring thirty-plus years of experience to the classroom. I had to figure out how to share the experience of investigative journalism, teach how to put an investigative story together, educate about the history and work of investigative reporters, all in three-hour segments over ten weeks.

"How do you do that?" I asked him.

"Lots of in-class projects. Don't worry. You're going to love teaching," Ron assured me.

At that point, he was more confident than me that I could pull this off.

Now standing in front of my first class, I realized my dream was turning into a hard reality. I waited for someone to answer the question. *Please*, I thought, *someone just try to answer the question.*

A tentative hand went up.

"Yes? How is an investigative story different from a regular news story?"

"You're uncovering something."

"Yes. Like what?"

"A scandal."

"Yes. Good. What else?"

"Something deeper?"

"Yes. In depth. Good."

We were off. I made lots of mistakes that first semester: handling grading, expectations. My students hung in there with me as I figured out how to pace a three-hour class, make it so their heads didn't hit the desk out of boredom or fatigue, and successfully use the high-tech "smart board." They rewarded me with investigative projects about their school—their recycling program, on-campus drinking, a restaurant with a bad health report.

But that first night of teaching I left the classroom quite differently than I'd imagined. I wasn't kicking up my heels. I was drained, exhausted, and challenged, wondering if I could ever be good at this. What I eventually learned is that I had a lot to learn, and that the best teachers would be my students.

Of all my Firsts during the year, standing before my first class was one of the most pivotal. I knew this was a first step into a possible second career; a tryout. I could envision a different path in the future. When I saw a spark of excitement in some of my students about what they were working on, I felt fulfilled in a new way. I was motivated to learn to be a better teacher.

Sharing whatever special talents, skills, and knowledge you have with others is a First that will give back to you many times over. When you teach, you will learn. It doesn't have to be in a formal classroom. Think about what skills and knowledge you can share and make it a First. Or just get back in the classroom as a student and start soaking up new knowledge. Your brain will thank you.

Other Firsts Like This to Try

◊ Offer to mentor an intern or someone at work who's younger than you.

◊ Enroll in a class to "up" your work skills or prepare for a second career.

◊ Learn a new language. Plan a trip so you can use it.

Bake and Decorate a Cake from Scratch: Day 277

Seize the moment. Remember all those women on the *Titanic* who waved off the dessert cart.

—ERMA BOMBECK

When I was growing up, I thought all cakes started in a cake mix box. If there was a cake to be made in my house, I was pretty sure Betty Crocker had something to do with it.

Perhaps I would have caught on in high school if I'd taken home economics like all the other girls. But I wanted nothing to do with a kitchen, baking, or sewing or anything that hinted of a domestic life. I took typing classes, preparing to take Jane Pauley's place on the *Today* show and be the world's ace woman reporter. I could not imagine a life in which I might want to bake a cake that didn't come from a bakery. Nor could I imagine I might need to sew my own hem or button. (What an idiot.)

At age fifty-three, I'd still never made a cake from scratch and looked more like Lucille Ball in the kitchen than anything resembling a cook. So, my daughter, Alexa, thought it was quite humorous when she decided to sign me up for a one-on-one class to learn to bake a cake—one that wasn't in a box.

Alexa selected a real gem of a teacher for me. Lucy Reall is from the west coast of Africa. When it comes to baking, she's an absolute perfectionist. There's no fudging or guesstimating on ingredients, and I spent a good four hours in her kitchen learning there are no shortcuts in her cake world. To Lucy, Betty Crocker is the devil.

Lucy had me measure and mix. She showed me how to get the batter to sit evenly in the pans, cool it properly coming out of the oven, slice off the bottom of cake layers to make them nice and flat. But this was nothing compared to her enthusiastically strict and exacting instruction for decorating with homemade icing.

Lucy whipped up a huge batch for me to practice my continuous swirls, shells, and flowers.

I decorated her butcher block table.

"No, no, no," she'd scold. "More lift, small shells, practice, keep going."

It took me an hour to get one icing skill down well enough that she agreed to let me try it on the actual cake. In truth, I don't think she was satisfied at all but realized that after an hour my shells and flowers got sloppier and droopier instead of perkier and more uniform.

We poured a chocolate ganache on top of the buttercream vanilla cake. I took it home to eat with my family.

Holy smokes! This was no cake from a mix. It was fresh. It melted in my mouth. My husband couldn't stop eating it. We sat there with the cake on the kitchen counter with two forks, first slicing polite pieces, then carving up huge wedges to stuff in our mouths. Dear God, this was where real cake came from. Now I knew.

Today I wouldn't dream of bringing a cake mix into the house. As they say, you can taste the difference. I honestly didn't know making something so delicious from basic ingredients feels almost as rewarding as filing the lead news story of the day. Learning something you can actually use in your life and that pleases people around you is a fabulously fulfilling thing.

What lesson did you skip as a kid that you wish you could go back and take? What kind of cooking or home project do you wish you could learn to do yourself? These make great Firsts and expand your skills, experience, and knowledge. Make a list and get cooking . . . or, uh, baking.

Other Firsts Like This to Try

◊ Sign up for a cooking class: Italian, French, gourmet, barbecuing, desserts, baking, pastry.

◊ Make all new recipes for a week.

◊ Don't want to cook? Build something or learn how to fix something yourself.

Final Thoughts

I was told once by a historian that Benjamin Franklin learned and knew every bit of knowledge that was in the world in 1776. It was all in his head. I don't know if that's true, but hey, it *was* Ben Franklin. It's possible. Franklin was constantly taking that knowledge and trying new things, prolifically inventing and creating (libraries, fire departments, insurance, books, musical instruments, newspapers, experiments with electricity). He was obviously a genius, and part of his genius was that he never stopped wanting to learn and share what he knew, wherever he went. Franklin knew life is a classroom.

You don't have to be a genius or a scientific researcher to know learning leads to a more productive, interesting, healthy life, not just now but into old age. Follow your curiosity and your passions. Be like Franklin.

TIPS FOR FINDING LEARNING FIRSTS

- Take a class with a friend. Sometimes it's easier and more fun to take on something new with a partner and share the experience.

- Go to hear someone speak. Check the calendars of authors, politicians, artists, entertainers you admire and go see them in person.

- Take a college course online. Some are free.

- Learn from intellectuals online. Check out Ted Talks to hear from today's leading authorities on any subject.

- Learn how to do almost anything from videos on the web. Google "How to . . ." (fill in the blank) and you can find instruction on everything from "how to belly dance" to "how to install a toilet."

- Find a new puzzle for your brain. We shy away from games and puzzles we don't know how to do. Push yourself to do the opposite and pick up something that challenges you.

CHAPTER 7

Facebook Is My Facelift

Firsts That Update You

I had no clue how old and dated I sounded when I said "Facebook is for kids!" That's what I believed in 2009. Yet, at work I was being highly encouraged to enthusiastically post a profile picture on my own Facebook page and embrace social media as a new and vital communication tool.

"Why?" I pounded my desk. "Why do I need social media? I'm already social!"

On every level I turned my back on the new technology and digital communication coming at me: I fumed at interns trying to text me. "Pick up the phone, why don't you??? Just call me!! Why can't people have a conversation anymore?" I looked longingly at an old manual typewriter collecting dust on a file cabinet in the office. It looked so solid, sturdy, and dependable. How could you trust a laptop or cell phone to hold important files, notes, and contact information on stories we were working on? I wanted paper in my hand.

Who were they to tell me I had to change? I scoffed. I'd survived decades of dramatic changes in TV news. I started in the business before cell phones for heaven's sakes. I made the leap from typewriters to the first computers. I happily welcomed video after film. I easily transitioned from taped to "Live!"

I wanted nothing to do with the next generation of TV news tools. I was angry with anyone who tried to push me in the direction of the future. I was hoping all this "stuff" would go away and that everyone would come to their senses and realize the "social media blah blah blah . . ." they wanted me to work on was just some ludicrous passing fad.

When I think about this time of my life, it's actually painful. I hit a bottom that felt like depression. I wanted to cry. I'd come home from work and curl up in a ball. I knew I couldn't keep things "the same," but I had no idea how to move forward, adapt, and enthusiastically evolve again.

Meanwhile, my twenty-three-year-old daughter, Alexa, was passionately writing daily entries for a personal blog and working professionally for an online Hollywood entertainment website in L.A. I applauded her work, but I didn't see how it related to me. She was doing the backstroke in this sea of technology, while I felt like I was stranded in the ocean.

Along with encouraging me to start my *One Year of Firsts* blog, Alexa implored, prodded, and pushed me to "get with it." She wanted me to love and be passionate about what she loved. To her, all these new communication tools were wonderful.

It's doubtful I would ever have started my Year of Firsts project without my daughter beating me over the head to do it. But as I learned to upload video and photos to my blog, I was also updating my brain, my internal software. You might say Me 3.0 emerged. I could almost feel every new web and technology skill firing up synapses and connections in my stubborn mind.

Yes, I was updating my "personal" files with a slew of technology Firsts. It was tough to get rid of my paper calendar, to break down and buy something online. I had to have someone tutor me on how to use my cell phone. The learning curve to take classes online, or even figure out which three buttons I had to push to turn on the TV was frustrating at times. But, I was excited too.

This internal updating process didn't stop with technology Firsts. I needed overall updating; an external update, a makeover. I used Firsts to experiment with my look: try new clothes, hair, makeup. Friends helped me realize I'd been wearing the same things for years. I suppose it was part of my subconscious attempt to try to ignore and hold back all the change around me. Again, I thought, the style that worked for me for the last decade would always work for me. It wasn't easy to let go, but I had to retire my favorite beat-up black leather jacket, rundown shoes, and makeup I'd worn through my thirties and forties.

I also started updating my pop culture IQ. I'd considered reality shows, YouTube videos, rap, and anything I didn't immediately understand as something I didn't need to know anything about. I put a cultural snob wall around myself. Not *New York Times*? Not NPR? Not *60 Minutes*? I wasn't interested. I had no idea this was making me "old," out of touch. Some of my Firsts became about sampling what I was missing. *Jersey Shore*? Check. *Housewives of . . .* whatever? Check. Hair whipping and Dougie dancing? Check. Yep, I checked back in to what was happening around me.

This transformation didn't happen overnight, but day by day, First by First, a layer of dust fell off of me. It was still me, of course; just better. I stopped looking back. I started looking forward again. I came to appreciate Facebook and Twitter. I love texting. I can't live without my iPad calendar. My wardrobe has gone through an overhaul. I changed my hair. I feel back in step with the world.

Updating Firsts helped me to not just survive, but thrive through the upheaval of downsizing and management changes at work. No, I didn't look twenty years younger. But I had a fresh look, new skills, and a curiosity about technology and culture to add to all of my substantial life and work experience.

It doesn't matter how young or old you are. Anyone can get stuck and forget to update along the way. Twentysomethings keep wearing clothes from college. Young moms get stuck in mom jeans. It's not about growing up. It's about growing, refreshing yourself. If you are stuck technologically, it's all right to ask for help to cross the digital divide. Switch the channel literally and metaphorically. Let in some new images and sounds from the web, TV, and radio. Don't worry. The real you isn't going anywhere. You're just sweeping out the cobwebs so you and everyone else can enjoy the best reinvigorated real you again.

Learn to Put on Fake Eyelashes: Day 55

Beauty, to me, is about being comfortable in your own skin. That, or a kick-ass red lipstick.
—GWYNETH PALTROW

SOME SCIENTIFIC EVIDENCE
UPDATING IS IMPORTANT

- Need to find a job? Get on social media. In 2012, Jobvite did a survey finding 92 percent of recruiters out of a thousand polled used social media to find new talent; 73 percent said they hired a new employee via social media including LinkedIn, Facebook, and Twitter.

- Cheer up. The web is good for your mental health. A University of Alabama-Birmingham study shows retirees who use the Internet regularly are 20 to 28 percent less likely to be classified as depressed.

- It's how young you feel! Gerontology researcher Markus H. Schafer says, "If you are older and maintain a sense of being younger, then that gives you an edge in maintaining a lot of the abilities you prize." His studies find that keeping up with trends and activities that feel invigorating and learning new technologies indeed keep you mentally younger and more optimistic.

When I was young, I swore I would never color my hair, put stupid age creams on my face, or apply anything to my body that's fake (besides a schmear of foundation, mascara, and lip gloss). I was convinced that I would be an ageless goddess, perfectly content with gray hair, wrinkles, sagging body, and all. And anyone who submitted to plastic surgery was selling out. Boy, was I naive.

I didn't understand what I see so clearly now. Your hair might not be that pretty silver gray. Your brows and lips get thin. You can look tired even when you get that rare good night of sleep.

Enter fake lashes.

It took my makeup artist friend Carie Brescia time to convince me about the wonders of fake lashes. I watched her put them on all the talent at the station and thought, *That's crazy. Who needs more lashes? Certainly not moi!*

Still, every day Carie said, "Come on. Let me just put them on you. Come on, come on, come on."

"Nah, not me," I'd say. I couldn't possibly deal with any more beauty maintenance.

But one day she caught me in a weak moment. She was pushing those lashes hard.

"Ahhhhhh. All right." In less than a minute, I was glued and lashed up.

I looked in the mirror to see the miracle. I'm telling you, there is no mascara in the world that can do what a pair of fake lashes can do. Hey, some people feel like they have super powers with fake boobs. I just needed a pair of lashes.

I could be deceiving myself, like the guys who think they look good in those bad toupees. I don't know. And I don't wear lashes during the weekend when I'm just chilling . . . no makeup either.

But is it wrong to wear something fake to feel like you look better, more youthful, more rested? Am I just on a slippery slope of more fake stuff: too much Botox, injectables, and surgery?

For now, for a few bucks a week, completely removable lashes and glue seem harmless to me. I wear them like the lightest butterfly armor against the assault of time. I consider them a mini lift.

My only message in all this is: experiment. Play! Try something noninvasive on for fun. Do it to please yourself, no one else. And if you like it, wear it, flaunt it.

Other Firsts Like This to Try

◇ For once, let your hairdresser do whatever he or she wants.

◇ Try hair highlights, a new color, a completely different cut.

◇ Get a real makeup lesson with a professional makeup artist.

Throw Out My Little Black Book: Day 107

Old age is . . . a lot of crossed-off names in an address book.
—RONALD BLYTHE

I threw out my little black book and I was jonesing for it. Badly. I wanted its reassuring feel, its complete coverage of my life and the people in it. I even missed the leather smell of its covers.

In case you've never owned one of these books, I should explain that it was the precursor to digital organizers. Losing it would be like losing your cell phone today.

My book not only held all my contact and calendar info; it contained my secret news sources—the people I knew I could call for a quote or a bit of inside information. It was an archive of my past, with appointments long gone by and obsolete phone numbers of people who had moved on. *My entire life* was in that little black book. All right, it wasn't so little, and it was heavy, like a brick in the bottom of my purse. That didn't matter to me. I *loved* my little black book.

My LBB and I were very happy until *it* came along: the BlackBerry—that smartphone that, all of a sudden, everyone was carrying. I had one, but I used it as a cell phone and nothing else. But before I knew it, the people I'd worked with for years had dumped their day planners like so much rubbish and put all their personal data into their BlackBerrys. Overnight (or so it seemed to me) my colleagues and friends turned into email addicts with carpal tunnel in their thumbs from typing and texting on that microscopic keypad. I began to understand why some people called it the "Crackberry."

Not me. My LBB and I were very happy together. I took it to bed with me. Took it on trips. I tried to reassure it that I wasn't going to trade it in for a shiny electronic gizmo. My beloved book was familiar territory, like a house you know so well you can find your way around perfectly in the dark. I had no desire to trade up to a hip new condo.

My husband and coworkers weren't having any of it. They chided me for not knowing how to put contact information in my new BlackBerry. "Can your beloved little black book text, make phone calls, take pictures, or surf the web?" one person asked snidely. They lectured me about how much more productive I would be as a reporter if I used all the capabilities of the technology at my disposal.

I was unmoved. After all, my LBB couldn't mix margaritas either, but that didn't mean I was going to trade it in on a blender. But eventually, as my Year of Firsts went on and it became harder to imagine new Firsts, I came face-to-face with the idea: *Maybe I should make giving up my little black book one of my Firsts.*

Not long after that, I sat at my desk one afternoon, grumpily entering numbers from my book into the BlackBerry. All the while I was thinking, "What if this thing breaks down or wipes everything out, then what?"

"Make sure you back up everything in your computer," a coworker told me.

"Sure." I had no idea how to do that.

But once I started using the BlackBerry, I reluctantly admitted that there were immediate advantages. I felt more "with it." I could access a phone number and dial it with just a couple of button pushes. It didn't weigh as much as my little black book.

I see. I get it. I don't have to like it.

Now, I have more knowledge in the palm of my hand today than I did in an entire newsroom of reference books fifteen years ago. When I finally accepted that, I realized it was time to stop being scared of technology. After all, it's not the tools. It's what you do with them, right?

But I didn't throw my LBB away. It's hidden in a drawer with a bunch of old keepsakes. For me, it's a touchstone in the purest sense of the word. It sounds hokey, but it's my link to a simpler time when my profession was about newsprint and typewriters and old-school reportage, not laptops and bloggers and twenty-four-hour news machines. I know, I know, it's just nostalgia—a word that literally means "pain of remembering." The good old days are in the past . . . and they weren't always that good to begin with. Still, I'm not throwing it out. Maybe I'll show it to my grandchildren someday. I'll sit them down on my knee and say, "This is how we kept phone numbers. Look, here's something called cursive writing. Not an LOL in sight."

I didn't say some of these Firsts weren't painful. Just consider them growing pains.

Other Firsts Like This to Try

◊ Get rid of your paper calendar. Use a calendar on an electronic device like your cell phone, BlackBerry, iPad, or laptop.

◊ Read the newspaper online.

◊ Download a book on an e-reader.

Update My Shoes with Rocco: Day 257

Create your own visual style . . . Let it be unique for yourself and yet identifiable for others.
—ORSON WELLES

Rocco Giancaterino and I have been friends for over twenty years. That's how long he's been cutting my hair. He also isn't shy about telling me the truth.

"You're good at news, but you're bad at shoes," he said one day.

"What? Who is looking at my shoes?"

"I'm looking at your shoes!"

I admit I prefer to buy my shoes at DSW; the cheaper the better. In recent years, comfort has become much more of a priority too. If I find shoes that don't hurt my feet, I might even buy them in three colors. To Rocco, however, these are dumb reasons to buy shoes.

"A shoe has to be hot . . . and, girlfriend, your shoes are not! They're shot." He looked at my worn-to-the-nub heels. "Throw those in the trash."

I should also tell you, I hate going shopping. I'd rather have someone stick me with needles than go to the mall. And while I appreciated my dear friend being honest and telling me my shoes were a fashion faux pas, I wasn't inclined to do anything about it.

"Okay," Rocco offered. "This is an emergency. I'm taking you shoe shopping. I can't have you looking like this."

A week later Rocco was holding me by the hand and leading me to the shoe department in the Saks Fifth Avenue discount store. He was charming the saleswomen, and had them running all over the place looking for my size in "that fabulous boot, and this lovely black suede number and this two-tone."

"Now these are shoes." he announced, picking up a pair.

The shoes were unlike anything I'd ever worn: spiky, trendy, sleek-looking things.

"Do I have to be able to walk in them?" I asked.

"No!" Rocco tried to tell me the shoes were not for chasing people down the street. They were just for looks, again, a concept I wasn't quite grasping.

"So, let me get this straight. I'm going to take out my credit card and spend hundreds of dollars on shoes just to look good."

"Yes."

When Rocco found the steel-gray five-inch Badgley Mischkas with big bows on the heels on sale for half price, he went a little nuts.

"Oh my gosh. Stick your foot in this."

I squeezed. Picture Cinderella's stepsister trying to get into the glass slipper.

"Ouch."

"You are buying these! These are gold. You have no idea."

Rocco was right. I had no idea.

The next week, the shoe compliments started coming in. I didn't know people (other than Rocco) pay attention to your feet. I felt a little younger, a little hipper, a little wobblier, and a lot poorer.

I appreciate Rocco educating me on shoe style. Obviously, I needed updating, and I know that thanks to Rocco my feet are now acceptably fashionable when I'm in the studio, or at a speaking engagement or some nice function. That being said, while the Badgley Mischkas always get extra attention, I can only keep them on my feet ten minutes at a time. (I generally just take them off and carry them around.)

Meanwhile, I continue to wear shoes that Rocco would like to rip off my feet. It's a compromise.

Truthfully, everyone needs a friend like Rocco.

Every now and then you have to shake up your style. Try things on you thought you would "never" wear. Change it up. A makeup, hair, clothes, or stiletto update might be just what you need to help feel a little taller, fresher, and more confident.

◊ Have a "Freaky Friday." Let your kid dress you. You dress your kid.

◊ Wear a color you never wear.

◊ Eliminate anything more than a decade old in your closet.

Cyber Shopping Monday: Day 334

Thank God we're living in a country where the sky's the limit, the stores are open late and you can shop in bed thanks to television.
—JOAN RIVERS

You'd think someone who hates going to the mall would love shopping online. Yet, I resisted. I just didn't trust it unless I could touch it: feel the sweater, try on the shoe, sit in the chair, or otherwise test whatever it is that I wanted to buy.

My daughter, on the other hand, casually buys and sells online regularly. She doesn't know why I torture myself, driving to the mall to get one special eye shadow when I could just go cyber shopping and have it delivered. I'll tell you why. Because (1) I don't have to wait for it to be mailed to me; (2) I know, despite the hassle of shopping, I'll get exactly what I want; and (3) I won't suffer anxiety wondering if someone has stolen my identity online.

I know, I know. It's an age thing. To my daughter, I'm the equivalent of the little old lady who doesn't trust banks and stuffs money under the mattress. I'm suspicious of it all and firmly believe in getting in the car, using lots of gas to drive everywhere to get everything. All right, maybe the kids have a point.

Cyber Monday is some crazy online sales day created by retailers to get you buying more things online. It pained me, but I decided I should throw caution to the wind, find a cyber coupon, and buy something insignificant for a First.

I went to a website called Shopforsparkles.com. I'd met the woman who started the business and knew she had some cute jewelry but had never bothered to check it out. Easy. I quickly found a little inexpensive necklace and matching earrings. I had a cyber coupon. I ordered three; one for me, two for gifts. I cringed, though, filling out my credit card information. *What horrible financial disaster would befall me now?*

I waited for something bad to happen. Instead, twenty-four hours later, a package arrived at my door.

What? How could this be? There was the jewelry I ordered, just as advertised. No rip-off. No financial meltdown. *Huh.*

Even after this successful First in what I'd perceived as the treacherous world of cyber shopping, I was slow to adopt it. Today, I'm more fully engaged.

Now, I do order my eye shadow online. I buy gifts online and have them shipped. I even ordered a whole set of outdoor furniture ONLINE! (That was a real leap.)

In the back of my mind I keep thinking, *It's too good. It's too easy. What's the catch?*

But I also know sometimes, you just have to take a leap and

shake off habits and attitudes that keep you mentally in the decade of disco balls. And if you really miss your disco ball, I'm pretty sure you can buy one online.

Other Firsts Like This to Try

◊ Downsize. Try a tablet computer.

◊ Make a bid in an online auction.

◊ Sell something online.

I Whip My Hair Back and Forth: Day 326

The aging process has you firmly in its grasp if you never get the urge to throw a snowball.
—DOUG LARSON

I can hear you right now saying "Really? You whipped your hair back and forth? And that's important, why?"

First (for those of you who don't remember this important moment in cultural history), in 2010 Willow Smith, daughter of actor Will Smith, had a big hit song called "I Whip My Hair." This was accompanied by a music video of the ten-year-old whipping her hair around kind of like it was a lasso being swung from her head.

I would have probably been completely oblivious to this short cultural hair-whipping frenzy if not for my daughter, Alexa, challenging me to "Try it!"

That night, we competed in our attempts to whip our hair like Willow. In the end, my hair just looked whipped. But, we were laughing. From now on, Willow Smith's song will always be included in my vast catalogue of useless, silly information.

I have to say I felt kind of cool knowing I gave hair whipping a whirl. I put this in the same category as watching *Jersey Shore*, voting for my favorite *Dancing with the Stars* couple, and doing the Dougie (dance).

Is it important to know who Snooki is? It might be if you want to get the punch line of a *Saturday Night Live* joke. For me, I like to know what everyone's talking about and feel left out when I don't.

I started to realize during my Year of Firsts that this cultural updating is as important as reading the paper or watching the news. Being "with it" means staying up to date on trends, fads, silly songs, dances, popular YouTube videos. It means I have to occasionally turn the radio station from NPR to Power 99. It means being curious about life. . . . *What's everybody up to?*

We often reject things that don't relate to us and our "oh so serious" selves. It dates us. Trying new fads, dipping into pop culture, is an easy First that will bring you back into the conversation going on around you. And the truth is, you don't know what you're missing that you might really enjoy.

Now, put your back into it, throw your hair into a ponytail, and toss your head around like you're Linda Blair in *The Exorcist*. I promise, hair whipping will not make you smarter, but it will make you more interesting.

◊ Listen to electronic dance music. Check out a rave.

◊ Watch a reality show you've sworn you'll "never" watch.

◊ Watch a competition singing or dance show and vote for your favorite.

Final Thoughts

You can wear your hair the same way you did in college, refuse to get a smart phone, never watch television, and be perfectly happy. But if you're not, if you feel stuck and isolated, it may be because you need to update your life. Be honest with yourself. Is fear keeping you from moving forward? It's okay to ask for help to cross the digital divide, update your style, and improve your pop culture IQ. Let Firsts be your excuse to try things you've only thought about before. Give yourself permission to experiment with new looks. Expose yourself to new ideas, music, videos, art. Be patient with yourself when learning new technology. Some Firsts will require daily changes, new habits, to make them part of your refreshed, engaged life.

TIPS FOR FINDING FIRSTS THAT UPDATE YOU

- Swallow your pride. Everyone of every age has to ask for help sometimes to learn new technology. Most are happy to share what they know. Start learning new technology you'll potentially use and incorporate into your life. Love books? Try an e-reader. Want to see your family on the other side of the country? Learn to Skype. Like games? Play Scrabble with your mom online.

- Take small steps. You don't have to throw out your entire wardrobe or chop off your hair. Buy one new piece of clothing that's a different style for you. Make small adjustments to your makeup and hair as you start updating your outer self. See how it feels for you.

CHAPTER 8

Catching Fireflies

Firsts for the Kid in You

In the summer of 1964, my best friend Jo Ellen and I sat on my front doorstep strumming toy guitars and singing "I Want to Hold Your Hand" so the whole neighborhood could hear us, though no one wanted to.

We were eight years old. Jo Ellen was long-legged and blue-eyed. I was short, pudgy, and "brown as a berry," my dad would say, from all the sun. And we were inseparable, running together outside with my sweet collie dog Cuddles in our little suburban Indianapolis neighborhood.

Our days were filled with some new doll called Barbie, dancing through the lawn sprinklers in bare feet and shorts, making forts in the woods, rolling in the grass, and spinning till we were dizzy. Cuddles would follow us, and we'd dress her up and teach her how to shake hands and roll over.

After dinner our moms would let us play Mother May I on

the driveway under the streetlamps. We'd see who could catch the most fireflies in our cardboard boxes with air holes in the lids. Then we'd release them blinking brightly away in the summer night.

Everything about that summer was new, fresh, and alive. Each day was an unpredictable adventure. I suppose that's the way things are when you're eight.

I don't remember summer ending, but I remember that next winter I learned about life and loss in that way that forced me to not be a child anymore.

My Cuddles, pregnant with puppies, was struck and killed by a car on a cold, snowy night. I cried for days and was inconsolable for weeks as I tried to come to grips with the awful reality of what happened to my sweet, constant companion. My child's world felt like it caved in for a while.

Soon after, my family moved from Indianapolis to Atlanta. I can still remember feeling as though my heart was torn out of me having to say good-bye to Jo Ellen.

I adjusted of course, made new friends, got another dog. Still, that summer remains in a perfect mental time bubble for me: my last weeks of blissful innocence.

If you are lucky, you had summers like that as a kid. You played that hard, and laughed so long tears rolled down your face. But we eventually leave childhood behind as we learn about the realities of life. Play is replaced with school and work and responsibilities.

One day you wake up and realize you can't even remember the last time you "played." As we get older many of us forget how to do it. Sometimes we're so out of practice and uncomfortable with play we turn away from anything that takes us back to the time we could innocently blow bubbles or stare up at the clouds while lying in the grass.

Is it too painful? Too sweet? Is it because our adult brain knows life is hard and unpredictable and we don't want to fool ourselves or waste time with childish things and memories?

And yet it's our inability to reach back and remember how to play that at times keeps us from moving forward, from laughing at ourselves and enjoying life.

When I set out on my Year of Firsts, I didn't intentionally plan on doing things I hadn't done since I was a child. But it soon became clear that anything I hadn't experienced in decades felt completely new and could be revisited as a First. And these childhood Firsts filled me with a joy I hadn't expected. So, I kept looking for more.

Climbing a tree, learning to Hula-Hoop, doing cartwheels, making driveway art with chalk, playing with all the toys in the toy store   all made me laugh and remember that it's okay to act like a kid again. In fact, it's not just okay to play, it helps put all the seriousness of adult life into perspective. Pure child-like fun inspires and gives us creative energy for everything else we need to do in our stressful, packed with to-do lists days.

If days and weeks go by without laughing, without games, without tapping into that secret we all knew about life as a child, the secret of play, then we are not fully enjoying our lives.

Dr. Stuart Brown, who has done extensive studies on play, has found through his research that adults who can reminisce about their happiest and most memorable moments can reconnect to what truly excites them about life. Brown's research also finds the most highly creative and successful people have a rich play life.

MORE SCIENTIFIC EVIDENCE OF
THE BENEFITS OF "THE KID IN YOU" FIRSTS

- Dr. Stuart Brown, the coauthor of *Play: How It Shapes the Brain, Opens the Imagination and Invigorates the Soul*, says research shows play is a biological necessity and adults who don't play enough in their life will demonstrate social, emotional, and cognitive narrowing. They are less able to handle stress and may experience "smothering depression."

- Be in the flow. In his well-known Experience Sampling Study, Mihaly Csikszentmihalyi found we are happiest when we are completely absorbed in an activity that involves effort and creative abilities and we are unselfconscious. That is often when we are "at play."

- Laugh some more. Numerous studies show laughing triggers feel-good endorphin chemicals in the brain.

- Keep laughing, because the American College of Cardiology reports laughing lowers blood pressure too, and the effects last forty-five minutes.

- Tim Brown, CEO of the innovation and design firm IDEO, says he's found "playfulness" results in some of the world's most creative solutions. Brown believes to create you need to have the ability to role-play and explore without fear of judgment from others.

So go sledding, build sand castles, fly a kite, and sing Beatles songs. Go back to your own sweetest summer and remember what you did. It's not too late to feel that spirit of adventure and spontaneity you naturally had when you were a kid. Give yourself permission and freedom to be silly and carefree for even a few minutes, and you'll be surprised how that will impact the rest of your day. Catch fireflies like you did when you were eight years old and feel the light go on inside your heart again.

Hula-Hooping: Day 31

Genius is childhood recalled at will.
—CHARLES BAUDELAIRE

I have to warn you. If you're a woman considering Hula-Hooping, understand if you do this in front of a guy, you might as well be pole dancing. Seriously! I only found that out *after* I took a Hula-Hooping lesson from Jennifer Rice. I'll explain later.

Jennifer sent me an email suggesting adult Hula-Hooping would be a perfect First for me. I told her I never could Hula-Hoop as a kid and that she shouldn't be upset if she is unable to get me successfully hooping. She insisted I must not have had the right motion down in third grade and she was sure it would take her less than twenty minutes to get me hooping like a pro.

Jennifer also promised she would not let me regress to my childhood memory of being the klutziest girl on the block, the only one who couldn't keep a hoop on her hips in the play yard.

On a Sunday morning I walked into a South Jersey dance studio, and Jennifer was waiting for me with a collection of brightly colored, sparkly ribboned hoops, much bigger than anything I remembered as a kid.

"Wow!" Now I was really doubtful.

"Don't get nervous," Jennifer said. "These are adult Hula-Hoops. You can do this."

Jennifer said she'd lost twenty pounds in one year just by Hula-Hooping every day. She put a hoop over her head, and pushed it spinning off her waist, smoothly turned and moved with the hoop going up and down her body, arms waving in and out like it was the most natural thing in the world.

"Wow," I said again.

"Okay, you try."

I picked a big red glittery Hula-Hoop out of her collection. Jennifer told me she decorates them herself and sells the hoops online.

"All right now," she explained. "Everyone thinks you move in a circular motion to Hula-Hoop but it's actually just back and forth or side to side."

She moved her body to show me. "See, that's it."

I promptly sent the Hula-Hoop flying off my hips and onto the floor.

"Wah. Just like third grade!"

"Well," Jennifer said, "you've got to move your core!"

It took a dozen tries. That's it. And then, like magic, the hoop was twirling on my hips. "Ha-ha. I got it!" I was completely tickled with myself.

"I could do this indefinitely, I think."

"You can, and it's great exercise. You can do this in front of the TV."

"Wow." I said it again. "Okay, I want one of these."

"Of course you do, Hula-Hoop girl!"

Later that afternoon, I walked into the house with my new Hula-Hoop.

"Whatcha got there?" My husband was very strangely interested.

"Oh, a Hula-Hoop. Want to see me Hula-Hoop?"

"I sure do." I was still clueless. I slapped that hoop on my hips and started doing a back and forth hip thrust as I'd been instructed.

I had Phil's full attention.

"Wow," Phil said, as I continued in an exaggerated undulation with my hoop swinging perfectly around my waist. He didn't even question it when I propped the hoop up against the living room wall . . . "just in case I feel like Hula-Hooping."

Months later I was getting ready to speak to a local women's group about my First experiences and decided at the last minute to bring my Hula-Hoop. I threw it in the back seat of my car and had almost forgotten about it until I got to a toll booth. The toll taker said, "Wow. Is that a Hula-Hoop?"

"Sure is!" I said proudly.

"You must be in really good shape!" He leered at me.

And that's when I realized that just the mere site of a Hula-Hoop in the possession of a woman can set a lot of things in motion besides your hips.

I stepped on the gas.

I shared the toll taker's reaction with the group, and the crowd howled. Afterward, quite a few of the ladies wanted to know, "Where can I get one of those?"

My Hula-Hoop is still resting against a wall in my living room. I have to admit I generally don't use it unless someone comes in the house and says, "Wow, is that a Hula-Hoop? You really Hula-Hoop?" If it's a girlfriend, I will gamely pick it up and demonstrate. It's good for a laugh. If it's a guy, I just wink and say, "Yep, I Hula-Hoop." I'm very careful with the power of the hoop.

But the truth is I have kept the Hula-Hoop out and visible as a daily reminder to myself to play, enjoy life, to step outside of myself and do something different and even quirky as often as I can.

Because what's life without some "Wow!" in it?

| **Other Firsts Like This to Try** |

◊ Play jacks.

◊ Try hopscotch.

◊ Skip rope.

Learn to Cartwheel: Day 174

My childhood may be over, but that doesn't mean playtime is.
—RON OLSON

I saw my yoga instructor friend Jennifer Schelter do a cartwheel once and I was immediately jealous.

'"How do you do that?"

"I don't know," she said. "I guess I just always have done it."

Ah, I thought. *She never stopped cartwheeling. How many things do we stop doing as adults?*

It occurred to me that my friend had a youthfulness about her that belied her age. Maybe because she still cartwheeled.

"Teach me?"

"Sure."

We met at a park with lots of soft grass for my cartwheel lesson.

"I think I used to know how to do this when I was ten," I said.

"Well," Jennifer laughed, "don't think about it too much. Give yourself a little running start."

And then she did one of her perfect, gymnastic-worthy cartwheels in front of me.

"Whoa. That's beautiful."

Picture two grown women practicing cartwheels in the park. (Or you can watch the video.) We were prancing around like kids. The sky was getting dark. Rain clouds were closing in. Jennifer was telling me, "Hurry. Do it."

My first cartwheels were "weanies." I was afraid of straightening my legs. I looked like I was doing some weird bunny hop. I couldn't fully commit to briefly supporting my body upside down while on two hands.

"I told you, stop thinking so much. Just feel it. Throw yourself into it." Jennifer was cheering me on. "That's it. You're getting there."

Jennifer showed me her "easy" cartwheels again, challenging me now in the way kids challenge each other at the fifth-grade lunch table.

"Can you get your legs up?!"

"Okay, okay, here I go."

And there it was, a bona fide cartwheel. "Ha-ha-ha." I jumped up and down.

"I'm going to do it again."

Boom. Again. I did it.

Jennifer did a cartwheel to celebrate too. Her cartwheels are long, graceful, and elegant like her. My cartwheel was a snappy little quick thing like me.

Raindrops started to fall, and we lingered a few minutes to dance in them.

When did we decide we were too old to cartwheel or roll around in the grass? If you have kids, stop just watching them play, get in there. You do it too. You get points for trying. Give your "adult rules" a time-out. Hang with friends who like to "play." It's contagious.

Other Firsts Like This to Try

◊ Spin until you get dizzy.

◊ Roll down a grassy hill.

◊ Lie in the grass and find shapes and people in the clouds.

Driveway Chalk Art: Day 229

The reluctance to put away childish things may be a requirement of genius.
—REBECCA PEPPER SINKLER

There is something very raw, spontaneous, and juvenile about driveway chalk art. It's our childhood graffiti, isn't it?

As a kid, I had to get permission to transform our driveway with a box of colored chalk. It generally turned into a mishmash of pastel flowers, rainbows, hearts, and hopscotch boards.

But as an adult I felt a little baffled now looking at the box of colored chalk I bought myself. Here, I'd given myself permission to draw anything I wanted on my own driveway and had no clue what to do.

Of course, when we're kids, we don't hesitate. We just started to create. You didn't worry about what the neighbors would think—whatever popped into your head was okay. Do you remember how you could completely lose yourself in space and time and feel like you were working on a world masterpiece on that concrete canvas?

I stared at my driveway awhile, considering all the possibilities, and made an adult decision: Marketing. Driveway marketing. A First within a first. Chalk art and a driveway ad. *Genius*, I thought. I began sketching out the letters of my website, luanncahn.com.

Unfortunately, I found my chalk skills were lacking as much as they were in elementary school. Indeed, it took no time for it to look like a small child had had her way with my driveway. I completely underestimated the chalk and space I needed for my project. Some letters looked squeezed in and much smaller or thinner than the others. Too late now. I couldn't walk away from it half done, though I wanted to.

I spent a couple of hours on my knees or hunching down on the driveway filling in five-foot-tall letters as fast as I could. You can imagine the stares from the nearby bus stop and drivers passing by. I'd smile, but how could I explain myself? I didn't try. I just accepted their "crazy lady" look.

It didn't matter, because after a while, I zoned out, thinking, strangely enough, about what people put on their tombstones. I'm not sure how I made that mental leap except I guess you could say I was putting a message on stone. Then I decided I was making a "living stone." What do you put on your living stone? (I swear I wasn't doing drugs. I was inhaling a lot of chalk, though.) As I worked, I wanted to start over. Erase everything. Ever the adult; editing. Why didn't I write something more inspirational?

Later, when I was done, I looked outside and saw dog walkers come by and pause, trying to see what was there. It was pretty rough.

A couple of days later it rained, and the colors all ran together on the driveway. Honestly, I was relieved. It wasn't like when I was a kid and the rain washed away the sunflowers and ponies I was so proud of. But it occurred to me the beauty of driveway chalk art is that eventually you get a clean driveway again. You get to start over. The driveway waits for another "work of art" or even a "living stone" message.

Many of the mistakes we make in life aren't permanent errors. Most of the time you can take another crack at it. We know that as kids. We forget that as adults. Sometimes starting over is just remembering it's rained, and you just have to get your box of chalk out and try again.

Other Firsts Like This to Try

◊ Finger paint. Seriously therapeutic for whatever ails you. Go ahead. Make a mess.

- ◇ Play with clay, ceramics, or Play-Doh.

- ◇ Do a paint-by-numbers kit. Remember those? They're still around.

Climb a Tree: Day 245

So, like a forgotten fire, a childhood can always flare up again within us.
—GASTON BACHELARD

Yes, it's a little risky to climb a tree when you are a fifty-three-year-old woman, and yes, I got some very strange stares when I did it, and yes, I really could have injured myself. Still, I'd do it again in a heartbeat.

I've always had this romantic notion about climbing trees, probably because my parents would never let me do it. You know how that is. It had been on my list of Firsts from the beginning of the year, and I was getting antsy to cross it off.

An opportunity came along on a beautiful sunny day when I had a scheduled interview in a park. I packed jeans and tennis shoes with me to be prepared in case I actually got to go on this dreamed-of tree climbing expedition.

Mike Spatocco was my photographer that day. I told him my plan.

"After I interview this guy, I'm going to try to climb a tree."

"You're what?"

"Yeah, climb a tree. Will you help me?"

He didn't seem sure about my sanity and worried how we would explain to our boss if I fell and broke a leg or something.

Finally, he offered. "Okay, it's been a while, but I've climbed lots of trees. I'm pretty good at it."

Mike was good at it. After the interview, he walked around the park with me and found what he thought was a perfect climbing tree. In thirty seconds, he'd pulled himself up to the first branch and went up several more.

"See? The hard part is just getting to the first branch."

I gripped the first branch like he showed me, threw my legs up on the trunk, and tried to pull myself up.

"AHHHH. URGH." No amount of straining and grunting and pulling was getting me up that tree.

Mike demonstrated several times, but I clearly didn't have enough upper body strength. Mike offered to push me up.

"Eh, I don't think so. I don't want to cheat." (Weird. I had some tree climbing rules I just made up.) "I think I need to find a tree with a lower branch."

We started looking. There were lots of big beautiful trees in this park, but all the branches were up high.

I walked toward some trees near the lake, and there it was. A tree for me. I could tell the first lovely thick branch was just low enough for me to get a little piece of my foot up on it. It took a few tries, but I finally was able to do a kind of jump-pull to get myself up.

The tree stretched out over the water, and I stopped to look at the gorgeous panoramic view of the park. I stepped up to another branch, holding tight, and then up to another level. I was probably fifteen feet off the ground.

"Ah. This is great."

Mike yelled, "Can you go farther?"

"Hmmm. Don't think so. The branches are getting thinner up here. Think this is it."

Boy, I thought, *I really did miss out as a kid.* My heart was racing with excitement. I loved being in the leafy branches.

A few people in the park were watching us. I thought maybe we were about to get in trouble, that some park ranger would yell at me to "get down from there." But no one did. We always knew as kids that adults can get away with everything fun!

I wanted to hang out in the tree for a while, but we were on a deadline and I had to make this adventure quick. I saw Mike was getting nervous too.

"Okay, I'm coming down."

"Go slow," Mike warned.

I did, because coming down, it was a little trickier to find my footing.

Mike coached. "Okay, you got it. A little to the left. Now lower yourself. The branch is right beneath you. I made a last little leap to the ground.

"Mission accomplished!" I announced.

Mike and I high-fived.

"That was awesome."

I know it sounds corny, but the tree climb elevated my day. Just the anticipation and the planning simply made me happy. As adults we forget how to dip into our inner child's sense of fun and adventure sometimes. We need to remember what it feels like to take those little risks that make us feel fearless. Kids who climb trees probably feel like they can take on the world. Remarkably, I can tell you it still feels the same as an adult. "I'm the queen of the trees!"

◊ Try skateboarding.

◊ Go to a park and play on everything you can: the swings, the monkey bars, the slide, the merry-go-round, and the sandbox.

◊ Learn to dive again or swim underwater in a pool.

Play with All the Toys in the Store: Day 252

If you carry your childhood with you, you never become older.
—TOM STOPPARD

If you've raised kids, then you probably know what it's like to have a house immersed in toys. Maybe because our daughter, Alexa, was an only child, Phil and I were recruited more often than not to sit down on the floor and play Trouble or Pretty Pretty Princess, or to jump into a game of tag with her friends.

When did all that play end? Was Alexa twelve? Thirteen? I just know at some point I packed up all the games of her childhood and put them in a box in the basement. I have to admit, there wasn't as much laughter and fun in the house.

One day, on our way to an assignment, photographer Bobby Ertel and I passed a Toys "R" Us. I hadn't been into a toy store in years.

"Hey, when we get done, let's go in that toy store on the way back," I told him.

Bobby laughed. "Okay, why?"

"I need a First today and I have an idea."

I've worked with Bobby a lot over the years. We're the same age. He laughs easily. He was more than willing to participate in anything fun.

We finished our work with just enough time to spare on the way back to the station.

"Come on." I urged. "Let's play." We went into the toy store and I headed for the toy guns and doll sections.

I picked up a space rifle that made wild noises and had red flashing lights that flowed up and down the barrel when you pulled the trigger. Bobby picked one up too.

"PYEW! PYEW! PYEW!" The toy guns were loud. "Alien shootout in aisle one!" I yelled.

That's all it took for two grown adults to start playing like eight-year-olds and laughing and looking for "more fun stuff."

"Ooh, look at this doll. It talks when you move it. . . . Oh, this one makes a funny face and giggles."

Bob picked up a Barbie doll. "What happened to Barbie?" he asked, staring at it. "She looks like a Victoria's Secret model."

"Yeah, I guess they updated her. I miss the black eyeliner and blue eye shadow."

We moved to the bike aisle. I found a tricycle and started scooting around on it to the next aisle. Bobby was laughing and shaking his finger at me like a tattletale brother. "Ooh, you are going to get in trouble."

But the store was practically empty. We hadn't seen a single salesperson. A mom shopping with her young daughter laughed when they saw us coming, me on the trike.

The little girl immediately engaged me and said, "Come try this. This is a car! It's my favorite." She led me to a pink girly motorized toy car.

"Okay. I might have trouble squeezing in it."

"Try, try!" she urged.

Bob was shooting a little video on my flip cam and joined in. "Yeah, Lu Ann, see if you can get in it."

It was tight, but I managed to get my behind in the seat and not break it. Everyone clapped.

We'd been running around the store and laughing for twenty minutes when I sensed we'd just about pushed the limits, and that the store manager would spot us soon. Time to go.

Bobby and I talked the whole way back about our favorite games and toys we'd played with as kids and the games we played with our own kids. We talked about missing "play" sometimes.

I thought about some of the new young startup companies I'd visited recently for news stories featuring Ping-Pong tables and basketball hoops and toys in the middle of their workplace. I'd judged it as being something frivolous from a generation that didn't take work that seriously.

Maybe I was wrong. Maybe the twentysomethings just intuitively understood more than our generation that "recess" isn't just for kids. What if play does make us more productive?

All I know is that Bob and I felt refreshed and reenergized after our "toy break," and when I got home, I dug out some old toys and challenged my husband to a game of Boggle.

When was the last time you played a board game, picked up

a toy or puzzle, ran around like a kid? Find a friend or family members to join you in play. You'll be surprised at how light and happy a half hour of play will make your whole day. Schedule a recess today.

Other Firsts Like This to Try

◊ Play a board game you played with as a kid: Chutes and Ladders, the Game of Life, Twister, Clue, Monopoly.

◊ Did you do big jigsaw puzzles as a kid? Pick one out with a thousand-plus pieces.

◊ Have a game night at your house. Ask friends to bring their favorite games and spend the night laughing and playing.

Final Thoughts

Every year at our family reunion on the beach, I take charge of the sand castle building day. Nieces and nephews I might see just once a year enthusiastically sit down next to me with buckets and shovels and we dig and build and laugh all day. They know Aunt Lu Ann will play in the sand with them.

What they don't know is that I probably get more out of it than they do. I get to be a kid with them, help decide if we are going to try to create a mermaid or a SpongeBob sculpture or "the biggest drip castle ever!" It has to be a First, so we do something new. The best part is I get to bond and connect with them in a way that is always special.

Research shows play is bonding. Whoever we share a laugh

with is someone we feel closer to. I get to know the next generation in my family in those hours we play together, and every year we share pictures and memories of what we made together in the past. Play makes us social, brings us together with others.

All work and no play? It's true . . . it "makes Jack a very dull boy." And it makes us less productive. Make play a priority and see how your outlook on everything changes for the better and sparks unexpected creative solutions in other parts of your life.

TIPS FOR FINDING PLAY FIRSTS

- Ask your friends who have regular poker, bridge, mah-jongg, or card games if you can join and learn how to play.

- What's new at the toy store? Find a new game that no one in your family knows how to play. Bring it home and let everyone help read the directions and learn together for the first time.

- If kids in your family have organized play, ask if you can join in. Get down on the floor with them and roll the dice.

- Be the play leader. Fly a kite, build a sand castle, play touch football, a game of catch, bubbles.

- Always say "Yes" to any organized sport or new game, even if you think you have no interest in it. Play anyway. Don't resist fun.

CHAPTER 9

The Weird and the Wacky

Firsts You Probably Won't Do Again

"Oh no, why?? Such a good idea gone terribly wrong!"

I'd been warned about Chatroulette. In 2010, it was brand-new, an Internet social network that allowed you to chat live through the camera in your laptop with people from around the world. Doesn't that sound wonderful? The website connects you randomly to others on the network. You can hit the Next button at anytime if you don't like the conversation, and someone else will pop up. I thought this sounded like a great First to try.

My first live chat was with two young women from London. After a very brief hello, they basically hung up on me without saying good-bye. Rude! They were obviously looking for something else on Chatroulette, something perhaps a little stranger that talking to a middle-aged woman in Philadelphia.

Then, I got connected to some bloke from Canterbury, England. He was overly cheery and after a brief discussion assured me he would "keep his clothes on." From the way the conversation was going, I doubted that.

NEXT!

Up popped a naked guy sitting in chair in a weird pose, looking like he was about to expose himself.

"Well, hello," he said.

NEXT!

But every random Chatroulette connection after that was the same. More naked men. More weirdness.

NEXT! NEXT! NEXT!

Apparently, it doesn't matter the country; I saw a smorgasbord of men of every ethnicity and age doing kind of the same thing. A live camera on the Internet, it turns out, is a great way for guys to "reveal" themselves to the world.

So much for Chatroulette. I was disappointed.

I laughed about it the next day with my girlfriends, who chided me. "What did you think was going to happen, you goofball?"

"I don't know. I thought maybe it would be like finding a pen pal on the other side of the world."

"Were any of these guys cute?" my single friend asked. "If they were, I'm trying this tonight."

"Ha-ha. I don't know. I think I was too stunned to look at their faces. I can promise you it will be a first-time experience you won't forget."

It was also something I didn't need to try again. It was just wacky. And that's okay. The wacky and weird are just part of a well-balanced diet of new Firsts.

Why does it matter? Because, wacky and weird experiences are like little bizarre exclamation points in your life. They keep the narrative surprising and interesting. These are Firsts that will make you uncomfortable, and challenge your normal good sense for sure, but they don't have to be big or difficult.

One day I walked the dog around the block backwards. I know every one of my neighbors who saw me do that thought I was seriously deranged (except my neighbor Mary, who knew right away it had to be a First).

We shy away from the strange and different because "to just go with it" presents us with a big unknown. Would my dog be able to walk forward while I walked backwards? Yes. Though she understandably looked confused. Would I be judged as a lunatic? Who cares.

I loved these Firsts. I loved that they pushed me outside the lines of my everyday norm. I generally keep to the straight and narrow, but at a time when I was stuck, I knew I had to break some of my internal "rules."

Put your big toe outside the lines of the box you've put your self in. Promise yourself if a wacky or bizarre opportunity comes along you won't just outright dismiss it. Ask yourself, "What's the worst that can happen?"

Firsts are about making sure today is different from yesterday. See just how far you can stretch yourself beyond the everyday boundaries that make you feel safe and in control. Those boundaries often get narrower as we get older.

Don't judge it before you do it, unless it's illegal or could be fatal. Then judge.

Trust me on this. We all need a pinch of wacky and bizarre in our lives. We all need to know that we are not so predictable and that even you don't know what you're capable of doing next.

SCIENTIFIC EVIDENCE WEIRD AND WACKY FIRSTS ARE WORTH DOING

- Go ahead. Be weird. Scott Barry Kauffman, PhD, writes that reshuffling your brain by doing something like eating with your other hand, or moonwalking backwards will help you be more creative.

- A number of psychological studies show it takes a certain amount of "rule breaking" to be creative.

- Wear something bizarre or out of your norm. Researchers have found costumes and uniforms change the way you behave. The effect is called enclothed cognition. One study found students who put on doctors' lab coats became much more attentive and studious. Halloween costumes allow wearers to "try on" different personalities.

Chatroulette.com is still around, by the way. Go there at your own risk.

Sled Down the Rocky Steps: Day 41

In nature, nothing is perfect and everything is perfect. Trees can be contorted, bent in weird ways, and they're still beautiful.
—ALICE WALKER

It had been a long, stressful day in the live news truck we called Mini 5. Over a foot of snow had dumped itself on Philadelphia.

Neighborhoods remained unplowed. People were testy. Not much was moving except the city snowplows working overtime to dig angry taxpayers out of the narrowest streets.

I was beat. Photographer Greg Durgin and I had done a dozen live reports during the day and evening newscasts, updating the latest conditions from neighborhoods with the most problems. We were cold and wet. I pressed my fingers against the heat vent in the truck, trying to get them to thaw out. There was no hope for my frozen toes. All I could think about was getting back to the station and digging my car out of the ice and snow in the parking lot to get home.

It was dark on the Ben Franklin Parkway when I spotted a crowd under the lights at the Philadelphia Art Museum steps.

"What's going on?" I said out loud.

"They're sledding the Rocky Steps," Greg answered.

"Really? I've never seen that before."

"Well, it only happens when we get a huge snow, deep enough to cover the steps so you don't go bumping down."

The famous Rocky Steps (from the *Rocky* movies) are laid out in about six tiers that lead up to the art museum. In this snow, it looked like a wonderful, steep, undulating sledding hill.

"Let's go," I told Greg.

"You're going to try this?"

"I need a First today. I can't think of anything better."

"You're going to kill yourself."

We parked and watched for a minute. Mostly college students were flying down the steps, slamming into each other on pieces of plastic, cardboard, all sorts of homemade sleds. It was a party on the steps.

"You don't have a sled," Greg reminded me.

I got out of the truck. A group of twentysomethings were standing around taking a break.

"Hey, I was thinking of trying this," I said. "How is it?"

"Ah, man. It's fun. It's fast. It will take your breath away. Here, take this."

One of the guys handed me a yellow piece of plastic.

"Just sit on it. Hold the bottom half up between your legs and scream."

I handed Greg my flip cam to take some video and started up the stairs with my borrowed "sled."

I decided to stop at the top of the bottom tier of steps, which is still a nice long run. I sat down on the plastic and was glad I had about ten layers of clothes on. My butt was well padded. How tough could this be?

Greg was at the bottom. "Okay. Come on down!"

I hesitated. It looked a little scary. The kids were whizzing by me. I realized it was more dangerous to sit in the line of traffic coming down from the tiers above me.

"Freezing down here, slowpoke!" Greg yelled.

"Okay, Okay!" I yelled. I pushed off.

It was a slick, steep ride down. . . . AHHHHHHHHHHH. I plopped in a heap at the bottom.

"Look out!" someone yelled.

Two kids crashed at my feet as I jumped out of the way.

I picked up the plastic and returned it to the owner.

"Aren't you going all the way to the top?"

"You know, I think I'm going to pass on that. I think I got a really good feel for this." I rubbed my aching behind. I stood back for a minute and continued to watch the nighttime sledding party.

As crazy as it was to participate in this madness, I wasn't tired anymore. I wasn't cold. My heart was pounding. I felt flushed and alive.

"That was really nuts, you know," Greg said.

"Yeah, I know. Good nuts. Thanks for hanging in there with me."

I ended a hard day of work with a little play, a little risk, a little wacky. And, once again I learned just when you think you're too exhausted to do one more thing, that's exactly when you should do one more thing—something fun, surprising, something that takes your breath away.

Other Firsts Like This to Try

◊ Take a class in Parkour, the art of using cityscapes to roll, vault, and leap.

◊ Dance in the rain until you're completely soaked and spent.

◊ Go skinny-dipping.

Eat a Scorpion: Day 195

When life hands you lemons, don't make lemonade. Make orange juice because being different is good.
—ANDREA FINICAL

The little white package arrived on my desk at work. I didn't have to open it to know what it was.

The return address said Phoenix. My former work partner Dave Bentley had moved there and warned me he was sending me a First: a dead scorpion to eat! BLAAH!

I love food. I will eat almost anything put in front of me: frog's legs, snails, gator tails, buffalo. But I've always drawn the line at insects. No chocolate-covered ants, bees, or bugs.

I wasn't sure what shape or form this scorpion would come in and was somewhat relieved when I pulled a large yellow lollipop out of a padded envelope. A big 'ole scorpion was preserved in the middle of that sucker.

Hmm. I looked at it from all angles. *I think I can handle this. At least it's not just a raw scorpion.*

The interns in the office gathered around me.

"Ooooh, what is that?"

"I think it's going to be my First today."

"You're going to eat that?"

"Yeah, I think so. Get the camera. We should document this for posterity."

I thought, *All I have to do is chew and swallow. Maybe I won't even taste the scorpion with so much sugary sucker around it.*

I took a small bite of the sucker, nibbling at the edges of the "prize" in the middle. I was thinking maybe I could just kind of bite off a small piece of the scorpion, you know, like a little leg or arm.

But noooooo! Of course the whole insect thing came off in one large bug chunk in my mouth.

The interns cringed.

Crunch. Hmmm . . . I tasted banana lollipop.

Another crunch. Nothing yet . . . chew, chew, chew . . . AHHHHHHH! There it was. It was too late to spit it out.

Yep, I got a really good solid taste of scorpion. No wonder they put it in a sucker. You need lots of sugar to help this go down.

What does it taste like?

Kind of metallic with the consistency of cardboard.

Gross.

I called Dave to "thank" him for his contribution and told him he could watch the video in my blog as proof the scorpion was delivered and devoured.

"What else you got out there to eat? Rattlesnakes? Cactus?"

He laughed.

"Nah. Just lots of scorpions. I saw it and knew it would be a good First for you. You ate the whole thing?"

"Accidentally, yeah!"

More laughter from Phoenix.

Anyway, I survive to tell the tale. (Speaking of tails, the poisonous scorpion tail was not included. Just thought I should tell you that in case you are considering this First.)

Am I a better person because I ate a scorpion? Nope. But it added a little extra something memorable to my day. That's it. Sometimes that's all you need.

Other Firsts Like This to Try

◊ Any weird chocolate-covered insect will do. Pretend you are on one of those crazy reality shows and eat a bug.

◊ Try some edible flowers. Throw some daisies and dandelions in your salad.

◊ Go to a weird festival in your area celebrating something offbeat like kudzu or scrapple.

Smoke a Cigar: Day 240

I used to think anyone doing anything weird was weird. Now I know that it is the people that call others weird that are weird.
—PAUL MCCARTNEY

Forget Monica Lewinsky and the rumored cigar incident with President Clinton. I've always thought smoking cigars seemed sensual. I don't smoke. I generally hate the smell of cigarettes. Still, one whiff of a cigar has always sent me reeling. There's something forbidden and mysterious in that lovely scent of musty, earthy, and sweet.

Smoking my first cigar was on my to-do list. The problem was, I didn't know any real cigar smokers that would help me out. I just kept that First idea "in my back pocket" until fate brought me to Cigar Cigars, a smoke shop in Horsham, Pennsylvania.

"Stop!" I told my photographer. "Pull in there."

I ran inside the cigar store, and my senses were immediately overwhelmed with that intoxicating smell.

"Hi there. Can I help you?" the manager called out from his smoke-filled office.

"Yes, I'm going to smoke my first cigar. What do you think?"

"Wonderful. That's a wonderful thing."

"How many women smoke cigars?"

"A lot, including my wife."

I didn't see another woman in the store. I peered through the heavy haze in the air and spotted a group of guys sitting around a table in a back room looking like they were having a great time.

"You ever smoke cigarettes?" the manager asked.

"Never."

"Good, because this is different. You don't inhale."

Visions of Clinton again. "Okay, no inhaling."

The manager took me to a room with hundreds of boxes of cigars.

"Any idea of what you'd like to try?"

"None at all."

"I'm going to start you on something mild and sweet."

And before I could say "Monica Lewinsky," he had the cigar cut and lit. Something called Romeo and Juliette. Very romantic.

I felt like a nervous schoolgirl doing something I thought I shouldn't. I puffed. A delicious swirl of smoke filled my nostrils. Heaven.

I made my way to the guys sitting at the back table.

"Mind if I join you? This is my first cigar and I don't know what I'm doing." (If that's not a good entrance line, I don't know what is.)

I was warmly welcomed to "the Breakfast Club"; Chuck, Howard, Jim, and Jeff told me they meet here for lunch every day. Not sure why they called it the "breakfast club." Maybe they just woke up. Anyway, they were happy to tutor me on the art of smoking cigars, and blowing smoke rings. (I know, I know. Don't say it. I told you there is something about cigars.) I'll admit, I felt very flirty during my virgin smoke because I knew I'd entered the inner sanctum of the male bonding room.

The guys told me this was one of the best parts of their day, talking, joking, socializing, helping each other solve business problems. The cigar smoke wafted above us in clouds.

And that smell. Ahhhh. I *was* inhaling.

The atmosphere was more than warm and friendly, but I had to go back to work.

"Thanks for the cigar lesson."

"No problem. Come back any time."

I never went back, but I still have what's left of that cigar. I tucked it away in a little spot behind a cookbook in the kitchen. Every time I see it I think maybe I'll light it up, even if it's old. But for now, I smell it, see if I can catch a whiff of that sweet aroma.

I'm sure smoking cigars is not a good thing for you. But just that once, I enjoyed my little indiscretion. In the right circumstance, I could be enticed to try it again.

Sometimes, you have to break your own rules (assuming it's not immoral or illegal or terribly harmful). I think smoking a cigar falls in that category. What is on your "break the rule" list that you've wanted to try? Give yourself a little leeway and go there for a First.

Other Firsts Like This to Try

◊ Ever tried warm brandy, sake, or ouzo? (Don't go overboard here!)

◇ Hookah bars are gaining popularity. Try it with a group of friends.

◇ Have dessert for dinner. Have dinner for breakfast.

High Heel Race: Day 268

All forms of madness, bizarre habits, awkwardness in society, general clumsiness, are justified in the person who creates good art.
—ROMAN PAYNE, ROOFTOP SOLILOQUY

I was inspired by the Heel A Thon in New York City. I saw the news story clip of hundreds of women leaving common sense behind and racing each other in the streets of NYC in their high heels.

"Finally," I said to my coworker Aditi Roy, "a race I could compete in."

Aditi is an avid runner and was cohosting the *10! Show* with me that week.

She's also about twenty years younger.

"In fact, I have an idea. . . ."

"Oh no . . ." Aditi knew what was coming.

"Come on. Let's have a high heel race after the show."

Aditi wasn't so sure this was a good idea. She'd need to be convinced.

Maybe it was because she knew I was a superstar runner in heels. I've been running on three-inch spikes since age twenty-one. This is part of the art of being a TV news reporter. Over the years, I learned how to run down entire city blocks in stilettos like I was wearing my best sneakers. I have chased down suspects, convicted politicians, and all sorts of scam artists in good high heels.

Now, someone in New York acknowledged it was a skill worthy of a legitimate race. Okay, maybe legitimate is overstating it, but I was thrilled to see the Heel-A-Thon let others of "my kind" show off this underappreciated talent.

Aditi reluctantly agreed to a race. We both prepared, looking at our personal collection of shoes for the speediest and sturdiest heels.

TV style fashionista and shoe maven Lillianna Vasquez offered to be the time keeper and judge at the finish line. We decided, in the name of sanity and to reduce the risk of twisted ankles, to keep the race indoors on a long carpeted stretch of hallway in the station.

I heard the Rocky music in my head as we stood side by side, poised to launch at the starting line. I was wearing a pair of dependable navy stilettos with gold heels that I knew I could fly in. Aditi went with a sturdy chunky-heeled strap number.

Lilliana raised her arm. . . . "On your mark, get set, go."

Aditi and I went toe-to-toe down the hallway. Despite her protestations, she wasn't going to give this to me. I had to put on some more speed. I felt my three-inch spiky heels pound into the carpet. *Don't fail me now, heels!*

I pushed a nose ahead of Aditi, crossing the finish line a nanosecond before her. The time? A thrilling five seconds.

Hey, don't laugh. One of the best track-and-field races at the Olympics lasts only ten seconds.

Whoo hooo! Aditi and I danced around, laughing, out of

breath. Okay, I was out of breath. She conceded defeat, happily. No ankles were injured. Our heels remained intact, and I confirmed that, indeed, my high heel running skill is my special super power.

What's your weird super power? Bring it on! Test your skills for a memorable First.

Other Firsts Like This to Try

◊ Enter yourself in any eating competition: pies, wings, hot dogs?

◊ Organize any contest: thumb wrestling, arm wrestling, Ping-Pong, horseshoes, stone skipping, grocery bagging, dishwashing.

◊ Celebrate weird national holidays like National Pillow Fight Day.

Running of the Santas: Day 352

Know what's weird? Day by day, nothing seems to change. But pretty soon, everything's different.
—BILL WATTERSON

Some women want jewelry. Some want furs. I just wanted a chance to wear one of those cute Mrs. Santa costumes. I know that's weird, especially since I'm Jewish. I must have some strange Santa envy.

I don't even know how to explain my irrational Santa wannabe thing, but I finally found the perfect excuse to indulge my fantasy: the Running of the Santas event in Philadelphia. Every year on a selected day before Christmas people dress in all manner of Santa attire and parade around the city streets.

When I told my husband I wanted to do this, it confirmed what he knew once again: I'm a little nuts.

"You know that's just a drunken pub crawl, right?"

"Yeah, but they look like they're having so much fun. I just want to dress up and walk around with them. It's also the same night as the TV station holiday party."

"You're going to the station party in a Mrs. Santa getup? Really?"

"Why not?"

We were headed toward the end of my Year of Firsts. Phil had gotten somewhat used to my crazy antics and knew at this point, once I got some notion in my head, there was generally no stopping me.

"All right, I'll go with you, but I'm not dressing as Santa," he said.

"That's fine."

Of course Phil was right. It was one big drunken Santa scene. Phil and I walked a few blocks with the other Santas in the freezing cold.

I was wearing the Santa dress of my dreams. It was red velvet with a white belt. White faux fur trimmed the deep V-neck, cuffed long sleeves, and the full skirt that hit me at the knees. I had a matching red velvet and white fur hat.

I knew it was silly, but it made me feel festive and happy to put it on. All right, and maybe once again, I felt like I was breaking some "rule": Jewish girls can't wear Santa stuff, but here I was and lightning wasn't striking me.

Phil took pictures along the way of the wild Santa outfits. People were laughing, falling down in the street. A half hour in, I was cold and had had enough.

We wound our way through a mob of inebriated Santas and some Philly cops trying to rein them in. We gratefully made it to the car without incident, and drove across the river to our station holiday party at the Adventure Aquarium.

My Year of Firsts had made me much bolder. I didn't think twice about coming into the party in my Santa dress. I just decided to own it. Everyone else was dressed in slinky dresses and suits, but it seemed like my costume just gave me license to be especially free and festive. I enjoyed every ho-ho-ho joke tossed at me from friends, coworkers, and people at the station I usually don't talk with. Nothing like a Santa outfit to break the ice.

During the night, I stepped out on the balcony by myself to get some air, and looked out on the Philadelphia skyline thinking about the fact that my Year of Firsts was coming to an end. I wondered what my days would be like without Firsts.

But then I laughed at myself for worrying even for a second about what might come next. I'd been at the same party a year ago feeling so stuck and unsure and uninterested. I never could have imagined the change in myself, the transformation and adventure before me, or that I'd be wearing a Santa dress for that matter.

I straightened out my Santa hat with the furry ball on top and walked back into the party, feeling confident and happy, knowing the end of my Year of Firsts wasn't the end of anything. It was just the beginning, the launch of many more Firsts to come.

Other Firsts Like This to Try

◊ Any holiday costume will do: pilgrim, Easter bunny, etc.

◊ Wear something unusual, different, and yes, maybe weird to a party or get-together.

Final Notes

Think back on a time in your life when you felt the most creative, the most open to new ideas, when you rebelled or didn't worry about conformity. All things were possible then, right?

They still are. No matter what your age, you aren't done yet. The most interesting, vibrant people you know continue to grow, evolve, and find new satisfying work and hobbies throughout their lives. They don't outright reject what may seem weird or bizarre. They stand out because there is a kind of "light" coming from them or energy that draws us in. They inspire us.

You've seen that spark in yourself before when you were full of fresh ideas, goals and soaking life in like a sponge. Reach back and tap into that person again. Don't reject "different" as something not for you. In fact, as an exercise in Firsts, go toward "different."

Push yourself to "go there" with a nonjudgmental mind, and don't be surprised when you find "the weirdest thing" makes you happy.

TIPS FOR FINDING MORE
WEIRD AND WACKY FIRSTS

- Check event calendars online or in the paper for anything offbeat: a Flugtag competition, a Renaissance Faire, a Color Run, or a butterfly release.

- Surprise yourself and break your internal rules a bit. Never wear a bikini or bright colors? Do it.

- Do anything backwards or out of order, just because.

CHAPTER 10

Good Karma

Firsts That Give Back

My father was a social worker and had one answer for every problem: "When you're feeling sorry for yourself, do something for someone else."

This always irked me as a teenager.

"But Steve broke up with me!"

My dad: "Do something for someone else!"

"I have a big pimple on my nose!"

"DO SOMETHING FOR SOMEONE ELSE!"

But it was my mother who hammered this lesson home with me, not by what she said, but by what she did.

We were living in Atlanta when my mother had to be rushed to the hospital for emergency surgery. She had been working full-time at a baby furniture store, running home every night to put dinner on the table for me and my two younger sisters and dad. But I'd been watching her health deteriorating for some time. She had ulcerative colitis, a disease that can destroy your large intestine. She could barely eat anymore without being in excruciating pain.

I was a kid in the early 1970s. I tried to pretend everything was okay and nothing was going on. But when I was told she had to have her entire large intestine removed and only had a 50 percent chance of surviving, I wasn't surprised. At that point, the disease had already taken over her life and ours.

It took months of recovery, but my mom survived the surgery that left her with an external ostomy bag to replace her colon. Some would have been devastated, but not my Mom. She had always been a beautiful woman and came back to life as weeks and months went by. She gained a little weight. Color came back to her face, and I saw an energy and vibrancy in her that I hadn't seen in years.

But then I witnessed the most remarkable thing. On weekends, after working long days during the week, she would get in the car dressed up to go on "visits." She didn't tell me what kind of "visits." She'd be gone for hours. She was a little secretive about it, and I wasn't sure she wanted to talk about it.

Finally, after watching her do this for months, I asked. She sat me down and told me there were other women who needed the same kind of surgery she had, but they were afraid. Sometimes, she said, they wouldn't leave their house, their bedroom, or the bathroom. My mom told me they'd rather live in the kind of extreme pain she suffered than have the surgery.

I remember asking if it was because they were afraid of dying from the surgery. And she said no, "It's because they are afraid of living with an ostomy bag." This stunned me, because to me my mom had never looked more alive and whole than she did right then.

I understood that my mom was doing something selfless for others, something she believed in. My mother had volunteered to show others there was life after this surgery. She would show these women her scar, her ostomy bag if they wanted to see. She looked healthy and strong and even more beautiful in my eyes when she told me about her "visits." And I thought, *I want to be just like my mom.*

Twenty years later, my mom held my hand in the hospital, as I contemplated an experimental new surgery to remove my large intestine. I was like my mom in a way that pained us both. Ulcerative colitis had destroyed my colon too. It had to come out.

I spent months in the hospital and endured two long surgeries, but in the end doctors put me back together with an internal pouch. Like my mom, I embraced life again. I could go back to being a wife and a mother and get back to the work I loved as a news reporter. I also knew, like my mother, I would tell my story to others privately and publicly through the Crohn's and Colitis Foundation.

And when I got breast cancer a year later, I would share that story too.

This was my mother's gift to me, the ability to share a personal experience to help others. And this sharing is part of my life.

There is a remarkable amount of research that indicates those who share and give and "do something for someone else" live longer, healthier, more satisfying lives.

The thing is, when you're stuck and unhappy, being told to "do something for someone else" seems like the most counterintuitive, insensitive advice and the last thing you want to hear. *How can I think of someone else when I'm so miserable? Why can't someone help me?*

I know this because I felt this way before I started my Year of Firsts. I knew I'd hit a wall because I wasn't helping anyone. I wasn't sharing anything. I shut down and turned inward.

Yet, from the first day of this unusual and quirky journey, as I ran into the ocean with strangers holding my hands, I saw what a relief it was to get outside of myself. Every First helped me leave behind the tired dialogue running over and over again in my head about my own personal issues and frustrations. I was able to open up my heart and mind again.

I needed to find new ways to share, new ways to give.

It was easy around the holidays to find first-time opportunities to volunteer. My experience at a homeless shelter tested me; wrapping Christmas gifts for needy kids filled me with an unexpected joy.

But Firsts that give back are something we can practice all year-round. It doesn't take a big commitment to take care of a stranger's bridge toll and "pay it forward." What does it take to give out free hugs for a day?

You can start with one hour, one gesture, one kindness, one positive intention for the day. Where can you lend your skills and your heart and your passion to help someone else or make their day better in some small way?

As soon as you start doing Firsts that give back, even if your initial motivation is selfish, your world will shift into a better place. There is a plethora of studies that show this is true.

SCIENTIFIC EVIDENCE GOOD KARMA FIRSTS ARE THE GIFTS THAT KEEP GIVING

- Giving makes you live longer. Stephanie Brown, PhD, at the University of Michigan found seniors who helped friends, spouses, relatives, and neighbors in some way lived longer over a five-year period than those who didn't provide any support to anyone else.

- Helping others may boost endorphins. A 2006 study at the National Institutes of Health found that when people give to charities, it activates regions of the brain associated with pleasure, social connection, and creates a "warm glow" effect.

- Giving IS better than receiving. A 2008 study at the Harvard Business School found giving money to someone else lifted participants' happiness more than spending it on themselves.

- Acts of kindness equal happiness. Sonja Lyubomirsky, at the University of California, Riverside, asked study participants to perform five acts of kindness each week for six weeks. All reported being much happier at the end of the study.

- Evidence of karma? Sociologists Brent Simpson and Robb Willer have done research suggesting generosity is likely to be rewarded by others down the line—sometimes by the person you gave to, sometimes by someone else.

- Generosity is contagious. Pass it on. A study by James Fowler of the University of California, San Diego, and Nicholas Christakis of Harvard shows when one person behaves generously, it inspires observers to behave generously and that is passed on to others by three degrees.

Today my seventy-eight-year-old mom is still giving by sharing her experiences. She recently testified before a congressional committee on Medicare and volunteers to lobby on issues that impact seniors. I know this makes her feel alive, happy, and fulfilled. Her example continues to inspire me.

If you're in a negative place, push yourself to take any small step in a direction that helps someone else. Mentally decide to put your situation on hold and put something good into the world. Something good will come back. Any act of kindness will boomerang with karmic energy. There's scientific evidence to support that too. Yes, really!

Pay a Stranger's Bridge Toll: Day 25

Kindness, like a boomerang, always returns.
　　—AUTHOR UNKNOWN

"Okay, so the plan is we're going to pay for the guy or woman behind us coming over the Ben Franklin Bridge."

I explained this for the third time to my work partner and friend Dave Bentley. He thought this was a ridiculous idea and was quiet as he drove our unmarked news car toward the toll booth on the bridge headed into Philly.

I kept yammering and handed him the money to pay our four-dollar toll and the toll of the car behind us.

"I can't wait to look back and see the expression on their faces."

Dave finally spoke, sarcastically. "Oh, I can't wait to see the toll taker. I have a prepaid E-ZPass, but instead you're going to pay our toll and the car behind us."

"That's not the point!"

I knew it made no sense. This wasn't about making sense. It was . . . well, it was an experiment. How does it feel when you commit a random act of kindness? I was giddy and happy to spend eight bucks to find out. But I could tell Dave thought it was a waste of money.

"Well, thanks for being my partner in this," I offered.

Dave: "I'm an unwilling participant."

I specifically told Dave this was an anonymous gift. But he pulled up to the toll booth and started talking.

"So listen," he said to the toll taker. "She wants to pay for the car behind us. Doesn't know who they are, but this is Lu Ann Cahn from Channel Ten . . ."

My jaw dropped. "No, no, don't tell them that! Don't say that!!"

Dave and I were now yelling over each other. The toll taker just grinned and said, "I'm sure the people behind you will appreciate it."

We drove through. I glared at Dave in disbelief. "Why did you tell them I was with Channel Ten?"

"So he wouldn't think I was crazy."

Dave was still obsessed with the idea that I spent four bucks on our toll when it was already paid for with the E-ZPass. But if we'd gone through the E-ZPass gate, I wouldn't have been able to pay for the car behind us.

I looked back. "Oh look, I think they're right behind us."

"No they're not," Dave deadpanned.

Who could tell? I couldn't see anything in the dark. I just had to imagine whoever it was was happy and surprised, like the time someone anonymously put money in my meter and saved me from getting a ticket, or the time someone handed me all their good Bed Bath & Beyond coupons in line because they had enough and wanted someone else to be able to use them.

Dave could tell I was disappointed he'd "outed" me to the toll taker.

"You know what?" he finally offered. "If anything, the toll-booth guy got a real good kick out of it. It at least made the tollbooth guy's day, and it definitely saved the guys behind us four dollars."

I laughed. I can't explain it. Despite Dave, the act of paying a stranger's toll just made me happy.

I hope maybe whoever crossed the bridge on my dime was inspired to do it for someone else and that someone else does it for someone else. I like the idea of random toll paying growing exponentially. Don't you? Go ahead. (Feel free to find a cheaper toll bridge than I did.) Make someone's day and enjoy the karmic ride.

Other Firsts Like This to Try

◊ Put an extra quarter in someone's parking meter.

◊ Randomly give a stranger a flower.

◊ Leave an anonymous positive message on someone's car or desk.

Give Out Free Hugs: Day 162

A hug is like a boomerang—you get it back right away.
—BIL KEANE, "FAMILY CIRCUS"

It was a sad day in the land of Philly: The Flyers had lost the Stanley Cup to Chicago.

I'd been waiting for a day to offer free hugs and decided this was the day. It's certainly not an original idea. I'd seen the story of Juan Mann, who created the Free Hug campaign when he found himself at a low point in his life with no one to give him a comforting squeeze. He made himself a crude sign that said "Free Hugs" and something kind of magical happened. Strangers came up to him for hugs, one after another.

There's a great deal of research that shows we as humans need and crave touch. A ten- to twenty-second hug can lower blood pressure and raise the pleasure chemicals in our brains. I thought faithful Flyers fans all around me might need that kind of mental boost.

At work, I sent out a station-wide email offering Free Hugs to Flyers Fans. After taping the *10! Show* in the studio that morning, I held up a cardboard sign for the audience offering them free hugs too.

Most just wanted a handshake from me. But then one lovely woman opened big meaty arms to me, and we embraced in a warm, long bear hug. The "hockey ice" was broken. Others stood in line for their hug.

I'll admit it's a little daunting to open yourself up to hugs from strangers. We aren't used to all this public affection even with people we know and love. And yet, once I hugged a few people, I know I felt the love. I felt . . . well, happier.

I went back to the office, and photographer Jim Friedman came in for his hug. Then Jen, the intern from another department I didn't know. Our sports anchor, Vai Sikahema, sent me an email requesting a hug. I met him in the studio to deliver.

Will O'Donnell, my intern who had been tutoring me that season in everything I needed to know about his beloved Flyers, did not want a hug.

"Come on, Will. It might make you feel better."

"No." Will didn't want to be consoled. I was insistent. "Okay," he finally compromised. "You can hug me."

Will is over six feet tall. I reached up to give him a big hug. He grimaced.

I suppose the recipient must be open to receiving something good to get any benefit. As it turns out, you can't force a hug on someone.

In the end, the gift was mine. I was hugged all day by co-workers, friends, and complete strangers.

I went home and gave my husband a big, long hug.

"What's that for?" Phil said, surprised.

"I gave hugs out today and realized I didn't hug you today."

"Ah. Okay." He smiled.

We all need hugs every day. We all need to feel connected by a warm touch, sometimes more than we know. When you haven't been hugged in a long time, when you've been in a hug drought, one big honest-to-goodness hug is like a long, wonderful, refreshing cool drink of water.

When was the last time you gave someone a good strong hug, or received one? Try offering hugs, just because. Or if that's too tough, just ask someone to hug you. And if you really need an excuse to try this First in a big way, you can offer free hugs on January 21. Just tell everyone you're officially celebrating National Hug Day.

Other Firsts Like This to Try

◇ Let people cut in line and in traffic all day.

◇ Make amends with someone you haven't talked to in years.

Toy Run with Chrome Riders: Day 297

Four wheels move the body. Two wheels move the soul.
  —AUTHOR UNKNOWN

I'm a sucker for tattooed, rough-looking, Harley Davidson motorcycle-riding guys who shed tears talking about the toys they're about to deliver to kids in a hospital. Bryan Grygo is one of those tenderhearted leather-clad bikers.

Bryan persistently touched base with me to make sure I would go on the annual Toy Run with his Chrome Riders Motorcycle Club out of Mantua, New Jersey. He didn't understand. He had me at "Hello."

Bryan suggested for a First that I ride in a sidecar (like Robin attached to the Batcycle) in the Chrome Riders caravan to Cooper Medical Center in Camden, and then help deliver toys. I also agreed to help buy the toys.

It was a cold night in Cherry Hill when I first met the group of mustached, burly men you wouldn't want to encounter late at night in a dark alley. Bryan broke into a big smile and greeted me in the parking lot with a giant hug. "Thanks for coming. It means a lot."

"Sure," I said, "put me to work." In no time, I was given a cart, a list of games, and a budget of several hundred dollars. The Chrome Riders had been collecting money all year and divided it among the group to run through the store like Santa's elves filling the sleigh (in this case, a U-Haul truck).

Bryan explained the toys aren't just for Christmas. "If a kid gets chemo, if they get a spinal tap, if it's their birthday, they get a toy. It's not just now. It's all year long." He choked up talking about what it's like to see a sick child's eyes light up when they hand deliver toys the day of the toy run.

The Chrome Rider wives, children, and girlfriends also descended on the store en masse. Within an hour we had ten full carts going through checkout.

The day of the Toy Run was spectacularly beautiful. A police escort met seventy-five Chrome Riders at their Mantua Clubhouse. I climbed awkwardly into a sidecar attached to one of the lead motorcycles for one of the bumpiest, windiest rides of my life. Well, what was I going to do? I was honored to be unofficially dubbed Queen of the Toy Run.

It's pretty heady to be part of a fearsome-looking group of bikers, making a whole lot of racket and noise, thundering down Jersey's Route 42. Bruce Springsteen would have been inspired.

After a three-mile ride that felt like ten, the hospital greeted the long train of Chrome Riders into their front parking lot like the superheroes that they are. I learned that over the years they'd raised hundreds of thousands of dollars to furnish the hospital playrooms with TVs and video games, tables and chairs.

And then it was Christmastime in the hospital. I watched big bruiser biker dudes tiptoe into rooms where babies and toddlers had a dozen tubes coming in and out of them. They quietly set down toys on beds like they were the tooth fairy, trying not to be caught in the act.

All I could see were these men, hell-bent on making a difference. They planned and talked about this event all year. And this day was clearly the highlight of their Christmas.

The U-Haul truck was emptied, and seventy-five bikers (and me) hugged each other, shook hands, then hit the road, headed back to the clubhouse. You can't forget a First like that. The Chrome Riders will always have a special place in my "born to be wild" heart.

Are you already a member of a group that is involved in a charity? Don't sit on the sidelines. See how you can do more than donate money. Put your heart in it. What can you do as an individual that will make the world just a little bit better today? That's the start of making you a little better.

Other Firsts Like This to Try

◊ Be the leader of a team for a race, or team fund-raising event.

◊ Volunteer at a hospital or nursing home.

◊ Be a secret Santa to a family who needs help.

Serve Dinner at a Shelter: Day 332

If you can't feed a hundred people, then feed just one.
—MOTHER TERESA

Every other Saturday, for the last twenty-five years, three sub-urban families bring a homemade dinner to the Trinity Center Men's Shelter in Philadelphia. When I asked the Burling, Jac-quette, and Quirin families why they started this and why they continue, one of them just shrugged and said, "There are home-less people on the street."

Eric Burling is one of my former TV news interns and a friend of my daughter's. I asked if my family could join his on this Saturday night. I'd been to homeless shelters many times to cover news stories, but I was always the observer, never involved.

We met in the small church basement. About a dozen home-less men quietly waited while my husband, daughter, and I helped the other families set up a little buffet in a tiny make-shift kitchen.

Alexa was home from L.A. for the holidays and was put in charge of serving the chicken. I was happy she was with us this night. It was an unusual family outing and just made me feel good we were together in this small act of kindness.

Serving food was easy. But food is just a vehicle for what the families believe is their real mission. They each sit down and talk to the men during dinner, getting to know the regulars. There's real conversation. No preaching, no religion, just the of-fering of friendship and company.

I was encouraged to do the same. I'm not a shy person (as you know), but I felt awkward. The men scattered about at a few lunchroom-style tables weren't talking much.

"Hi," I said to a man who looked tired and worn from being out in the cold all day. I couldn't tell if he was old or young but just looked older. I asked if I could sit down with him. He looked up and nodded. I started eating.

"The chicken's good," I said. "My name's Lu Ann."

He didn't tell me his name. But slowly, a conversation began. He said he stays in the library when it's cold.

"It's nice in there," he said, "because there are books I can read all day."

He couldn't really say why he's homeless. He told me he doesn't want to be, but "can't quite figure it out." But he did tell me a hot meal and a safe place to sleep on a Saturday night is a blessing to him.

My family left with such mixed feelings. It wasn't just that we thought a warm meal and a place to sleep is so precious to so many. Instead, we *felt* it in a raw place that night, a place that hits your gut.

More than anything I felt grateful to the families who took this on as a mission in their lives. It's a kind of giving I know I'm not capable of right now. I wish I was. I admire it. Eric ended up leaving his full-time TV news job after this and working in a homeless shelter full-time. He says it's more satisfying to him.

All I know is that in a small basement in Philadelphia, every other Saturday night, the world is a little better because of the Burlings, Jaquettes, and Quirins. And that every once in a while we should try to emulate them.

◊ Work in a food pantry.

◊ Volunteer for Meals on Wheels.

◊ Introduce yourself to your senior neighbors and see if they need help.

Final Notes

The day I was scheduled to go wrap Christmas gifts for children as a First, I didn't want to go. I felt cranky. I felt tired. I'd worked hard all day and I just wanted to go home.

I had trouble finding the place in Center City Philadelphia where I was supposed to do this "good deed." I finally found a dark building where I was met at the door and taken down some creaky steps to a basement. I was doubtful my mood would change.

Then I walked into this brightly lit room that looked like Santa's workshop. A dozen people were happily crowded around a big table covered with bows, paper, and tape. There were shelves of gift-wrapped packages of every size, organized for every age. I didn't know anyone in the room, but they quickly pulled me into the group so I could help.

In a matter of seconds, I was smiling. My hands were busy wrapping and my heart was full. I was told by the Children's Crisis Treatment Network these gifts would go to children who probably would get nothing else for Christmas.

I no longer cared what nonsense happened at work. I wasn't thinking about my problems.

This is what these giving-back Firsts do for *you*.

Think about it? When was the last time you volunteered? When was the last time you did something for someone else, something for a stranger just out of the goodness of your heart? Even if it's the tiniest gesture, a promise to yourself to make someone else feel better today is an action that in the end will be the best gift you can give yourself.

TIPS FOR FINDING FIRSTS THAT GIVE BACK

- What is the one thing you've always thought about doing as a volunteer? How long have you been thinking of volunteering for Habitat for Humanity? Stop thinking and just do it. What is your passion? Your special talent? Where can you put that to good use? Is it reading? Volunteer to read to kids, or seniors in a nursing home? Is it house painting? One man recently made news by painting houses for free and inspired the whole town to help. Take your special skill and give it away to someone who needs it.

- Just do something because it's the right thing to do. Decide to pick up any trash on the street you see today instead of walking over it.

- The possible random acts of kindness are endless. Hold doors for everyone. Help someone you see struggling to reach something at the grocery. Give someone your seat. Share whatever you grow in your garden with your neighbors.

- Who do you know who needs a little extra help? Push yourself to reach out at work, at home, at school. Don't be afraid to get involved.

- What charities and events does your office or company become involved in? Sign up when they ask for volunteers. Combine a good deed with a good workout. Raise money and do a 5k walk/run to benefit a charity.

CONCLUSION

"How many of you are stuck?"

I was nervous as I stood at the podium before five hundred women at the Pennsylvania Women's Conference in the fall of 2010. I was leading a panel on "Reinventing Your Life."

I repeated the question as the crowd of women settled into their seats in the ballroom of a Pittsburgh hotel. It got quiet.

"How many of you feel stuck in your life, at work, or at home?"

It was the first time I'd posed this question in front of a large formal audience. I wasn't sure what the response would be. Just the fact that I'd been asked to speak at this conference was a First for me. The room was full of accomplished, smart entrepreneurs, moms, professionals, and students of every age from across the state.

After a few seconds, I was stunned when I saw nearly every

hand in the room go up. At the same time, it confirmed what I'd suspected: I'm not alone.

Women told me they were struggling with their business, loss of a job, a major illness, aging parents, empty nest, divorce, marriage, death, and just change in general. I heard lots of versions of "stuck."

Women who came to this seminar wanted to know about this personal experiment of mine: daily Firsts. How did it work? Were things changing? Did I feel better? What did it accomplish?

Today I can tell you.

The journey through my Year of Firsts required me to be extremely present in the moment, to remember the joy in fresh and new experiences, to remember even a change in "addee-tood" was a choice within my control.

My world went from a small box of daily predictable events to what I now envision as a large circle with expanding ripples, intersecting with other circles that continue to grow and spread in all directions. My brain hums with all the new projects, relationships, interactions, and events my Year of Firsts put into motion.

For now, I have returned to my first love, news reporting. But it's different. Embracing new technology and social media has changed and enhanced the way I do my job. It wasn't easy, but updating my skills through Firsts allowed me to not just survive but thrive in a work environment that is still evolving as I am.

But beyond my career as a news reporter, I just see an open door with all sorts of possibilities. Firsts set me on a new path that includes more teaching and writing and opportunities for creativity that make me happy.

I continue to say "Yes" whenever I can and jump at the chance to do something I've never done before. Firsts are part of my life now, something I consider a healthy habit.

And most importantly, I don't feel stuck. That's what "Firsts" did for me.

Meanwhile, I can't wait for you to read the words I'm writing now and for you to find something here for *you*. I can't wait for you to discover one new thing that starts to change where you are today.

I implore you. I dare you. . . . Hula-Hoop and eat weird things and roll in the mud and climb a tree. Do the Hokey Pokey and turn yourself around. Dance in the rain, go to the opera, and bang on the drums. Help your neighbor. Skype with your kids, find your high school sweetheart on Facebook, and get a smart phone. Don't wait. Do it.

Challenge your fears. Push yourself out of your comfort zone. You don't have to run away from home to change your life. You *do* have to do something different. No one can do this for you. Stop waiting for someone to save you, or for some circumstance out of your control to change. The change must come from you.

I know. You say, "I don't know where to start." Start with Day 1 . . . one new thing you've never done before. I DARE YOU!

May the Firsts be with you.

MY YEAR OF FIRSTS

A List

2010

1. Polar Bear Plunge
2. Read Every Word in the Newspaper
3. A Day Without a Mirror
4. Analyze a Dream
5. Learn the Alphabet Backwards
6. Don't Say Anything Negative All Day
7. Eat Desserts All Day
8. Buy a Lottery Ticket
9. Reconcile Longtime Family Issue
10. Brush My Dog's Teeth
11. Keep the Car Clean
12. Day Without Coffee
13. Phil's Sixtieth Birthday
14. Blog for Haiti
15. Learn to Tell a Joke

16. Talk to a Stranger

17. Use My Own Bags for Groceries

18. Donate Blankets

19. Go Back to School

20. A Day Without Cursing

21. Hang Upside Down

22. Donate Blog to Charity

23. Play Racquetball

24. Walk Five Miles Through Woods

25. Pay a Stranger's Bridge Toll

26. Voice a Nonprofit Video

27. Walk Across the Ben Franklin Bridge

28. Learn to Fence

29. Improvisational Dance

30. Go to the Movies by Myself

31. Hula-Hooping

32. Eat Vegetarian

33. Be a Clown

34. Knitting Lesson

35. A Day Without "CrackBerry"

36. Watch *Jersey Shore*

37. Make Snow Angels

38. Make Chicken Wings

39. Row Exercise Class

40. Create and Perform Rap

41. Sled Down the Rocky Steps

42. Eat Peanut Butter and Tuna Fish

43. Go to Forty-Third Floor in the Comcast Building

44. Meditation and Journaling Class

45. Kept out of Film Festival

46. Juggling

47. Try an E-reader

48. Shovel Horse Manure

49. Meet a Favorite Author

50. Eric Clapton at Madison Square Garden

51. Sing on Broadway (the Street)

52. Start a Daily Journal

53. Participate in a Chain Email

54. Meet the Damsels in Success

55. Learn to Put on Fake Eyelashes

56. Climb a Salt Hill

57. Solo Kitchen Dancing

58. Visit the Newseum

59. Walk to the White House

60. Power Plate Workout

61. Command My Cell Phone

62. Dominoes

63. Learn Song on Piano

64. Sing with a Community Choir

65. Dance at an Irish Hooley

66. Drive the Speed Limit

67. Go to Mexico

68. Massage on the Beach

69. Zip Line

70. Latin Dance on the Beach

71. Ride Zip Lines and Rappel into Cenote

72. Towel Art

73. Learn to Edit Video

74. Invite Neighbors to Dinner

75. Teach Old Dog New Trick

76. Indoor Rock Climbing

77. Yoga Wall Class

78. Interview "First" Expert

79. Airport Spa

80. Latin Wedding

81. Let Daughter Dress Me

82. Victim of Burglary

83. Treat Everyone Like at Five-Star Hotel

84. Fifteen-Minute Isometric Workout

85. Swing at Driving Range

86. Meditate Twenty Minutes

87. Acupuncture

88. Bake a Chocolate Flourless Torte

89. Save Cake Disaster

90. Download an App

91. Matzoh for a Week

92. Be a "Tree Hugger"

93. Chatroulette

94. Zumba Jam

95. Make Rack of Lamb

96. Plant a Potted Herb Garden

97. Adult Ballet

98. Organize Pantry

99. Walk the Dog Backwards

100. Put Quarters in Strangers' Meters

101. Go to Neighbor's Concert

102. Card Craft Workshop

103. Simplify Socks

104. File Consumer Complaint

105. Learn Spoon Trick

136. Make Friend's Reality Video Audition

137. Yoga for Living Beyond Breast Cancer

138. Sew a Button Correctly

139. Online Auction Bid

140. Go Down Largest Wood Slide

141. Eat Pretzel Cheesesteak

142. Walk to Work

143. Legacy of Love

144. Swing on the Trapeze

145. Win eBay Auction

146. Send Off Long-Time Work Partner

147. Cohost the *10! Show*

148. Use a Hands-Free Cell Phone

149. Learn Flyers Song

150. Drink "Green Monster"

151. Join the Venice Beach Drum Circle

152. Tarot Card Reading

153. Henna Tattoo

154. Getty Museum

155. In-N-Out Burger

156. Art Therapy

157. Design a Necklace

158. Fly with Wi-Fi

159. Absolute Truth All Day

160. Hockey School

161. John's Doggie Shop

162. Give Out Free Hugs

163. Roller Hockey

164. Mud Run

165. Make Almond Brittle

166. Launch Improved Blog

167. Help Accused Murderer Turn Himself In

168. Work on Chocolate Assembly Line

169. Drink a Red Bull

170. Feed the Stingrays

171. Celebrate Summer Solstice

172. Jump into Pool with Clothes On

173. Golf Lesson

174. Learn to Cartwheel

175. Ride a Segway

176. Cook with Food Network Star

177. Bicycle Taxi

178. Softball with Firefighters

179. Ride the Ducks

180. Letterboxing

181. Serve Cheesesteak on the Street

182. Play Classical Music All Day

183. Parade and Sing with Barbershop Quartet

184. Workout with Olympic Skater

185. Visit Please Touch Museum

186. March in Parade

187. Catch iPad Envy

188. Go to Adult Day Camp

189. Learn to Cut Glass for Mosaic

190. Screenings Under the Stars

191. Put Our Sweet Dog Angel to Sleep

192. Mourn and Share Readers' Thoughts

193. Go to Japanese Tea Ceremony

194. Interview Zac Efron

195. Eat a Scorpion

196. Ride in Race Car

197. Work at Rita's Water Ice

198. Play with Seals

199. Train as a Coffee Barista

200. Skype with Someone Doing Year of Firsts

201. Dance During Derriere Workout

202. Carrot, Broccoli, Spinach Juice

203. Shecky's Girls Night Out

204. Sushi Lesson

205. To the Roof of Philly's Tallest Building

206. Give a Horse His Shots

207. Angel's Ashes Come Home

208. Spend a Day in a Wheelchair

209. Ride with "Harley Babes"

210. Count Every Step

211. Make Quiche Lorraine

212. Eat Cheesecake Gelato

213. Learn the Phillies Starters

214. Climb Lighthouse

215. Feed Alligators

216. Surf

217. Bait and Fish

218. Fly a Two-Handle Kite

219. Drive an RV

220. Rent a Player and Movie for Plane

221. Pick Peaches and Corn

222. "Man Shower"

223. Make Pork and Tofu Dumplings

224. Bottle Cap Art

225. Make Ice Cream

226. Try Foursquare

227. Dunked by Young Readers

228. Three Movies in One Day

229. Driveway Chalk Art

230. Chi Gong

231. Learn Sign Language

232. Ride a Mechanical Bull

233. Shoot Hoops from Second Floor

234. Row on the River

235. Goddess Affirmation Card

236. Tie a Bow Tie

237. Go to Kid Movie Without Kids

238. Drive with No Planned Destination

239. "Blind" for an Hour

240. Smoke a Cigar

241. Soul Line Dancing

242. Play Laser Tag

243. Ride Go-karts

244. Take an Art Class with a Nude Model

245. Climb a Tree

246. Honey and Egg Mask

247. Learn Cool Handshakes

248. Flugtag

249. Cemetery Tour

250. Taste 18 Flavors of Ice Cream

251. Screen Print a T-Shirt

252. Play with All the Toys in the Store

253. Blow Shofar

254. Drum Lesson

255. Gay Bingo

256. Speed Shopping

257. Update My Shoes with Rocco

258. "Farmville"

259. Tofu Cheesesteak

260. Spin Basketball on Finger

261. Yom Kippur Services Online

262. Bury Angel's Ashes

263. Eat at an Ethiopian Restaurant

264. Walk Cynwyd-Heritage Trail

265. Teach Grad School

266. Rock Out with Hooter's Drummer

267. Drive the Fun Bus

268. High Heel Race

269. Free Museum Day

270. Personal with Porcupine

271. Light Pool with Candles

272. Throw Pizza Dough

273. Ice Carve

274. Change Windshield Wipers

275. TV Show Theme Song Trivia

276. Wear $18,000 Bracelet

277. Bake and Decorate a Cake from Scratch

278. Vote for *Dancing with the Stars*

279. Teach Mom to Skype

280. Make Gnocchi

281. Ultimate Frisbee

282. Work for the Interns

283. Parkour Lesson

284. Bake for Overnight Crew

285. Pose for Street Artist

286. Tread (Mill) for the Cure

287. Dine with Chef Eric Ripert

288. Speak at Pennsylvania Conference for Women

289. Learn Salt Shaker Trick

290. Design for Designer

291. Ballroom Dance and Craps

292. "Control TV" Reality

293. Draw with Animator

294. Reiki

295. Toy Run Shopping

296. Magic Baseball Mud Mask

297. Toy Run with Chrome Riders

298. Paintball

299. Ghost Hunting

300. Chicken-Eating Contest

301. Sewing Lesson

302. Croupier for Charity

303. Crash, Be Sick, Grade Papers

304. Ride Electric Bike

305. Pure Barre Workout

306. Tour Fortune Cookie Factory

307. First in Line to Vote

308. Tap Dance Routine

309. Battling Ropes

310. Help Judge Phillies Ball Girls

311. Volunteer at Shredder Event

312. Cake for Bake Off

313. Cake Boss Eats My Cake

314. Eat a McRib

315. Trumpet Lesson

316. Learn to Speak *Jersey Shore*

317. Baha'i Service

318. Poetry Reading

319. Audition for Roller Derby

320. Drive Zamboni

321. Do Pas De Deux

322. Geocaching

323. Get Key to Secret Closet

324. Surprise Birthday with Alexa

325. Bye to Paper Calendar

326. I Whip My Hair Back and Forth

327. Ultimate Pen Twirling

328. Sweet Potato Cupcakes

329. Cut Alexa's Hair

330. No Stress Thanksgiving

331. Black Friday Shopping

332. Serve Dinner at a Shelter

333. Search for Gravity Hill

334. Cyber Shopping Monday

335. Learn to Throw a Football

336. Yo-Yo

337. Primal Scream

338. Go to Comic Book Store

339. See Liberty 360

340. Drive Miniature Horse and Buggy

341. Museum of Jewish History

342. Gift Wrap Toys for Kids

343. Whistle Through Hands

344. Volunteer at an Animal Shelter

345. Cheer Friend at Bodybuilding Contest

346. Help Teen with Ulcerative Colitis

347. Surprise Furniture Contest Winner

348. Puppetry

349. Launch "Cliff Lee" campaign

350. Belly Dance

351. Do the Dougie

352. Running of the Santas

353. Paint Ceramics

354. Cut Down a Christmas Tree

355. Download an iTunes Song

356. Tennis Lesson

357. Skate at the River Rink

358. Eat Raw

359. Secret Santa Contest

360. Snow Building Contest

361. Take Racquet Ball to Achy Back

362. Cake in the Face

363. Chiropractor Adjusts Back

364. Eat at Le Bec Fin

365. Remember an Incredible Year

RESOURCES

Chapter One: Firsts That Overcome Fears

Dean, Ben. "Authentic Happiness." Newsletter, University of Pennsylvania. www.authentichappiness.sas.upenn.edu/newsletter.aspx?id=66.

Reynolds, Gretchen. "Phys Ed: Why Exercise Makes You Less Anxious." *Well* (blog), *New York Times*, November 18, 2009. http://well.blogs .nytimes.com/2009/11/18/phys-ed-why-exercise-makes-you-less -anxious.

"Scientists Find More Efficient Way to 'Unlearn' Fear." ScienceDaily .com. October 6, 2003. www.sciencedaily.com/releases/2003/10/0310 06064929.htm.

Chapter Two: Firsts for Busy People

Jaffe, Eric. "The Psychological Study of Smiling." *Psychological Science*. December 10, 2010. www.psychologicalscience.org/index.php/publi cations/observer/2010/december-10/the-psychological-study-of -smiling.html.

Parker-Pope, Tara. "Happy Couples Share New Experiences Together." *New York Times*, February 12, 2008. www.nytimes.com/2008/02/12 /health/12well.html?_r=0.

Waliczek, T. M., J. M. Zajicek, and R. D. Lineberger. "The Influence of Gardening Activities on Consumer Perceptions of Life Satisfaction." *HortScience* 40, no. 5 (August 2005).

Walker, Richard, John Skowronski, and Charles Thompson. "Life Is

Pleasant—And Memory Helps to Keep It That Way." *Review of General Psychology* 7, no. 2 (2003).

Chapter 3: Invitation Firsts

Cain, Susan. "When Does Socializing Make You Happier?" ThePower OfIntroverts.com (February 7, 2011). www.thepowerofintroverts .com/2011/02/07/when-does-socializing-make-you-happier/.

Ybarra, Oscar, Eugene Burnstein, Piotr Winkielman, et al. "Mental Exercising Through Simple Socializing: Social Interaction Promotes General Cognitive Functioning." *Personality and Social Psychology Bulletin* 34, no. 2 (2008): 248–259. doi: 10.1177/0146167207310454.

Unger, Katherine. "Rat Race Is Bad When Alone." *Science* (March 13, 2006). http://news.sciencemag.org/sciencenow/2006/03/13-01.html.

Chapter 4: Firsts That Move You

Maddux, W. William, Hajo Adam, and Adam Galinsky. "When in Rome . . . Learn Why the Romans Do What They Do: How Multicultural Learning Experiences Facilitate Creativity." *Personality and Social Psychology Bulletin* 36, no. 6 (2010): 731–741. doi: 10.1177/ 0146167210367786.

Reid, Robert. "Why You Should Visit a New Destination." CNN (May 24, 2010). www.cnn.com/2011/TRAVEL/05/24/visit.new.destinations .2011/index.html.

Chapter 5: Adrenaline Rush Firsts

Caprariello, Peter A., and Harry T. Reiss. "To Do, to Have, or to Share? Valuing Experiences Over Material Possessions Depends on the Involvement of Others." *Journal of Personality and Social Psychology* 104, no. 2 (2013): 199–215. doi: 10.1037/a0030953.

Gass, Michael. "Adventure Therapy with Groups." www.academia .edu/2399632/ADVENTURE_THERAPY_WITH_GROUPS.

Chapter 6: Learning Firsts

Howard, Beth. "Age-Proof Your Brain: 10 Ways to Keep Your Mind Fit Forever." *AARP the Magazine* (February/March 2012). www.aarp.org/health/brain-health/info-01-2012/boost-brain-health.html.

Cohen, Patricia. "A Sharper Mind, Middle Age, and Beyond." *New York Times*, January 19, 2012. www.nytimes.com/2012/01/22/education/edlife/a-sharper-mind-middle-age-and-beyond.html?pagewanted=all&_r=2&.

Chapter 7: Updating Firsts

Cotton, Shelia R., George Ford, Sherry Ford, and Timothy M. Hale. "Internet Use and Depression Among Older Adults." *Computers in Human Behavior* 28, no. 2 (March 2012): 496–499.

Jobvite Staff. "Jobvite Social Recruiting Survey Finds Over 90% of Employers Will Use Social Recruiting in 2012." Jobvite, July 9, 2012. http://recruiting.jobvite.com/company/press-releases/2012/jobvite-social-recruiting-survey-2012.

Schafer, Markus H., and Tetyana P. Shippee. "Age Identity, Gender, and Perceptions of Decline: Does Feeling Older Lead to Pessimistic Dispositions About Cognitive Aging?" *Journal of Gerontology: Social Sciences* 65B, no. 1 (January 2010): 91–96.

Chapter 8: Firsts for the Kid in You

Amber, "An Interview with Dr. Stuart Brown, MD Co-Author of Play: How It Shapes the Brain, Opens the Imagination, and Invigorates the Soul." *Catalyst Ranch* (blog), August 23, 2010. http://blog.catalystranch.com/interviews/an-interview-with-dr-stuart-brown-md-co-author-of-play-how-it-shapes-the-brain-opens-the-imagination-and-invigorates-the-soul/.

Brown, Tim. "Tales of Creativity and Play." Ted: Talks. Filmed May 2008, posted November 2008. www.ted.com/talks/tim_brown_on_creativity_and_play.html.

Csikszentmihalyi, Mihaly. "Flow, the Secret to Happiness." Ted: Talks.

Filmed February 2004, posted October 2008. www.ted.com/talks /mihaly_csikszentmihalyi_on_flow.html.

Gorman, James. "Scientists Hint at Why Laughter Feels So Good." *New York Times*, September 13, 2011. www.nytimes.com/2011/09/14 /science/14laughter.html?_r=1&.

University of Maryland Medical Center. "University of Maryland School of Medicine Study Shows Laughter Helps Blood Vessels Function Better." UMMC News Release, March 7, 2005. www.umm.edu/news /releases/laughter2.htm.

Chapter 9: Firsts You Probably Won't Do Again

Hajo, Adam, and Adam Galinsky. "Enclothed Cognition." *Journal of Experimental Social Psychology* 48, no. 4 (July 2012): 918–925. http://dx.doi.org/10.1016/j.jesp.2012.02.008.

Kaufman, Scott Barry. "Why Weird Experiences Boost Creativity." *Huffington Post*, June 5, 2012. www.huffingtonpost.com/scott-barry -kaufman/why-weird-experiences-boost-creativity_b_1568677.html.

Kuszewski, Andrea. "Creativity: A Crime of Passion." *Science 2.0* (blog), December 12, 2009. www.science20.com/rogue_neuron/creativity _crime_passion.

Chapter 10: Firsts That Give Back

Brown, Stephanie, Dylan M. Smith, Richard Schulz, et al. "Caregiving Behavior Is Associated with Decreased Mortality Risk." *Psychological Science* 20, no. 4 (May 2009): 488–494. www.rcgd.isr.umich.edu /news/Brown.Psych%20Science.May%2009.pdf.

Fowler, H. James, and Nicholas A. Christakis. "Cooperative Behavior Cascades in Human Social Networks." *Proceedings of the National Academy of Sciences* 107, no. 12 (March 23, 2010): 5334–5338.

Simpson, Brent, and Robb Willer. "Altruism and Indirect Reciprocity: The Interaction of Person and Situation in Prosocial Behavior." *Social Psychology Quarterly* 71, no. 37 (2008): 52.

Suttie, Jill, and Jason Marsh. "5 Ways Giving Is Good for You." *Greater Good* (blog), December 13, 2010. http://greatergood.berkeley.edu /article/item/5_ways_giving_is_good_for_you.

ACKNOWLEDGMENTS

With thanks and gratitude to:

Penny Nelson of Manus & Associates Literary Agency, who believed in and nurtured this project.

Jen Groover and Tim Vandehey, who envisioned a book before I did.

Perigee Books editor Meg Leder for lovingly guiding and editing my words.

TV news agent and dear friends Steve and Marsha Dickstein.

Loraine Ballard Morrill, who happily joined me and thought of so many Firsts.

To the inspirational cheerleaders on my journey: Mina Sabet, Karen Araiza, Tina Luque-Blacklocke, Bryn Freedman, Jennifer Schelter, Kelly Green and the "Damsels in Success," Jenna Stevens and Kathe's Krusaders, Jackie Morlock, Ashley Peskoe, Jami Osiecki Shore, Lori Wilson, Terry Ruggles, Jamie Broderick, Suzie Burmester, Vince Papale and Janet Cantwell Papale.

To my biggest First fans: Mary and Paul Ziogas, Jennifer Rice, Patricia Cianflone, Gail Ramsey, Jeanne Sailor-Ewe, Kristen Stewart, Shelley Laurence.

To friends who support all my crazy ideas: Dave and Connie Bentley, Dave and Fran Harrington, Andrew Glassman, Rocco

Giancaterino and Michael Sparano, Barb and Jerry Mark, Robin and Jeff Belack, Cindy and Steve Bell, Cindy and Andy Dahlgren, Laurie Berg Sapp, Ed Dress, the Mah-jongg Girls: Ruth, Fanny, and Hedy.

To Drexel University, the University of Missouri, and the Pennsylvania Conference for Women for so many learning and teaching Firsts.

To Living Beyond Breast Cancer, the Philadelphia Chapter of the Crohn's and Colitis Foundation of America, the Phillies, Comcast, the City of Philadelphia, the Aquatic and Fitness Center in Bala Cynwyd, and the Adventure Aquarium for offering so many First experiences.

To former NBC 10 managers Chris Blackman, Dave Parker, and Dennis Bianchi, who gave their blessing for this project.

To News Director Anzio Williams and General Manager Eric Lerner for their continued support.

For their unconditional love: my sisters, Terri Dinardo and Linda Evans; my mom, Carol Berman, and Ted Lefman; the Houser family; the Ablemans; Uncle Jerry and Aunt Evy; and my dad, Ron Cahn, who always said, "One day you'll write a book."

To Phil, who loves me through sickness and health and every dream I can dream.

And Alexa . . . my best First. This book would never be without you.